D1711855

Managerial
Breakthroughs
Action Techniques
for Strategic Change

Managerial Breakthroughs Action Techniques for Strategic Change

James R. Emshoff

amacom

A Division of American Management Associations

Library of Congress Cataloging in Publication Data

Emshoff, James R
   Managerial Breakthroughs

   Includes index.
   1.   Organizational change.   I.   Title.
HD58.8.E48   658.4′063   80-65873
ISBN 0-8144-5612-X

First Printing

To my wife Marguerite

Who makes our team what it is
and me what I am

Preface

This book is written from a management consultant's perspective on business. A consultant's view of an organization's management problems often differs somewhat from that of people who live the problems from day to day within the organization. First, consultants are hired to bring a broad range of experience to bear on the organization's problems, since the company's management faces a continuously evolving situation in which specific details and general principles seldom crystallize separately. Hence, the consultant seeks constantly to generalize from the problems he or she encounters in various client organizations. Second, the consultant tries to offer more than an immediate solution to the client's specific problem; he seeks to institute new management concepts and techniques that will undercut the chances that the same type of problem will reoccur in the future.

These two consulting principles—problem generalization and process orientation—are the bases upon which this book is organized. I focus on the fundamental problems that are generic to American business; that is, issues that will affect the success of both large and small companies in all industrial sectors during the 1980s. In addressing these problems, I don't provide specific solutions except by example; rather, I discuss how and why management concepts must change before executives can hope to deal more constructively, creatively, and efficiently with their problems on an ongoing basis.

Domestic as well as world economic and political events of the seventies have made unprecedented demands on America's corporate executives. As we lunge into the eighties, the infant decade promises little relief. I offer these perspectives in the hope that they will provide managers with new insights that will enable them to sail more gracefully on innovative solutions through the myriad issues and choices they face. But the final decisions of how to solve these problems will come from management, not from consultants. The challenges streaming toward business will make the eighties an exciting decade. My desire to participate more fully in these challenges and the changes they will assuredly demand have fired my need to shift gears in my career and join Campbell Soup Company.

Although I have left the consulting world and the academic environs of the University of Pennsylvania's Wharton Applied Research Center, I am now even more convinced that American business needs the input from groups that seek generalizations of management processes. We need to strengthen the partnership between management consultants and executives before we can accelerate the changes I believe are needed in management processes.

I must take responsibility for the specific content of this text. But the ideas it contains are largely the contributions of others. Corporate managers too numerous to mention have played key roles in testing and implementing these concepts, as have my many colleagues at Wharton. There are, however, several players whose roles in developing some of the book's major concepts have proved especially significant. Arthur Finnel and Ian I. Mitroff were instrumental in creating Strategic Assumptions Analysis, and R. Edward Freeman pioneered the Stakeholder Management process, both of which are addressed here.

I am grateful to the senior staff of the Wharton Applied Research Center for providing funds for the research and editorial assistance that enabled me to complete the book following my departure from the Center. In addition, the Center's Director of Communications, Kenneth McDonnell, improved the quality of the final product immeasurably by turning much of my complex jargon into simple English. The unenviable task of transforming handwritten text into a finished manuscript fell on the shoulders of Peggy Giannone at Campbell and Mary Ann Snedeker at the Applied Research Center. Only I can appreciate the task they faced.

JAMES R. EMSHOFF

Contents

Even if you're on the right track,
you'll still get run over if you just sit there.

—WILL ROGERS

1

Overview

Necessity, who is the mother of invention. —PLATO

"Pioneers get their wagons burned." So saying, the president of a diversified consumer goods company rejected the New Project Development Group's proposal to invest in a project that was highly speculative but, if successful, promised substantial returns. He hadn't accepted any projects from the group for nearly two years.

The president of one of the nation's top banks opened the annual planning meeting warily. "The theme of our management philosophy for the foreseeable future," he cautioned, "will be 'Snug Up.' Any activity that's not related to improving the efficiency of our basic banking business should be cut out if at all possible."

A large manufacturer of building materials has spent more than ten years working on a new product that has the potential to open significant untapped markets. Development has reached the point where a \$25-million capital investment decision must soon be made to test production feasibility on a pilot basis. If the capital is committed to the project, it won't be because projected rates of return are now estimated to meet acceptable criteria. That test had been passed long ago. Instead, the key to an affirmative decision will be the belief by corporate executives that the economic environment of the future will be "friendly."

The sentiments of these three companies are typical of those in today's business community. Considering the unstable economic climate business leaders have encountered throughout most of the seventies, such belt tightening is hardly surprising. When the leaders of business are convinced that the economic future is fundamentally sound, more expansionary thinking would undoubtedly *follow*. But the pivotal issue yet to be resolved is whether the United States can achieve lasting economic recovery without business taking the *lead* in fostering the resurgence. Are businessmen acting like sailors in a fleet of leaky boats, struggling against a strong undercurrent—some bailing furiously, others paddling upstream to keep their own boats afloat—while the entire fleet drifts toward a whirlpool that will eventually sink them all? Does the business community need a new game plan that will recharge it with more offensive power?

In 1976, my colleagues at the Wharton Applied Research Center and I became convinced that traditional management practices would fail to treat many of the ailments plaguing American business. We felt that fresh thinking was required among executive ranks to encourage greater innovation and renewed risk taking. We wanted to be able to offer specific alternative management approaches if the basic problems that worried executives during the 1974–1975 recession didn't recede.

Were we simply "ivory tower eggheads"? Hardly. Over the years we have worked as consultants to managers from a cross section of industry on specific strategic problems confronting their organizations. We have sought to develop and test fresh approaches to key business problems. Literally, the "real world" has been our laboratory.

This research strategy has worked exceedingly well. Through it, we have received quick—and occasionally painful—feedback on the value of our approaches. In many cases long-term relationships were established with clients, enabling us to experiment with our approaches in considerable detail. Some of the organizations that have been part of this effort are American Telephone & Telegraph Co., Anheuser-Busch, Inc., Campbell Soup Company, Cerveceria Cuauhtemoc (Mexico), Columbia Pictures, Exxon Corporation, Fidelity Bank, Johnson & Johnson, OKC Corporation, and Weyerhaeuser Co.

Working closely with such diverse companies has accelerated our progress because we have been forced to generalize our methodologies. As a result we have focused our attention on fundamental issues that are generic to American business. We still don't have comprehensive solutions to offer and probably never will, but many of the alternative management approaches for which we perceived a need have taken shape and have been used with great success.

This book deals with a variety of problems facing American business today, all of them reflecting one central belief: The key problems and opportunities confronting American executives in the 1980s will not be solved through conventional management practices. "Trying harder" simply won't work. We are going to have to "try different," by developing more creative decision-making approaches in the face of thickening pressures from many quarters to dilute business performance.

As of this writing, the clouds of concern over such issues as inflation, recession, energy, and government and foreign intrusion are even more disturbing than they were in the mid-1970s. Hence, in this era of world and domestic economic crises, executives ought to heed the call for a fresh look at these problems and for an examination of new approaches to solving them.

I hope to challenge executives to assess the fundamental principles upon which we manage. If these principles pass the test of objective scrutiny, they should remain in place. But if traditional approaches aren't getting the job done, we must try new ones. The proposals I shall offer carry with them the risks inherent in change. These alternatives must be assessed against the risk of standing pat.

Do we really need to change our approach to management? Let's first examine a few key strategic problems that directly or indirectly affect the viability of every American business.

Strategic Problems

Every private company must make a profit to survive. To do this, it must offer goods and services at prices that simultaneously (1) stimulate sufficient demand and (2) produce an acceptable return over costs of production. Daily, managers must deal with dozens of issues to enable the company to continue to perform this tightrope act. But beyond these operational issues lurk a number of strategic considerations that play an increasingly critical and complex role in business performance. These strategic factors—such as increasing government regulation, declining employee motivation, slowing technological innovation, and exploding consumerist activity—lack the dramatic impact of a large customer who cancels an order, a competitor who introduces a major new product, or a supplier who hoists prices substantially. However, these global factors have caused drastic shifts in all business operations and in the attitudes with which business leaders approach the future. Let's look at what's happening in these four arenas.

Government Regulation

To many businessmen the challenge of dealing with ever-increasing government regulation is the most significant strategic issue they face. Few executives are optimistic about disentangling themselves from government; it's like trying to stuff toothpaste back into the tube. Despite government efforts to deregulate a few industries, such as transportation, most industries face expanded regulatory controls with each passing year. Pressure from consumer and environmental groups for greater government intervention grows stronger all the time. And once the government steps into a new area—energy, for example—its involvement seems to expand like a cancer. Once established, the regulatory bureaucracy seems to generate its own growth and feed on itself.

The economic stakes of regulation are enormous; the costs of compliance run into the billions. In 1974, for example, Kaiser Aluminum & Chemical Company spent an estimated $5 million on labor and overhead costs to meet the paperwork requirements of the entire maze of government regulations. In the same year, Eli Lilly reported that it devoted more man-hours to paperwork than it did to research on drugs for cancer and heart disease.[1] The benefits? In dollar terms, nobody knows for sure.

The most frightening thing, however, is the rate of increase of these costs. In the early sixties, it cost $1 million and took up to five years to guide a new drug through the Food and Drug Administration's regulatory maze. This ordeal now costs $18 million and can take up to ten years. General Motors said it spent $190 million preparing and filing government reports in 1974 (mostly to the Environmental Protection Agency regarding compliance with federal emission standards). By 1978 that figure had spiraled to a whopping $3 billion, and required a staff of nearly 23,000. Despite the 1974 Commission on Federal Paperwork and assaults by Presidents Ford and Carter on the problem, the intrusion of the federal government into the personal lives of the public is growing, with the burden falling most heavily on small businesses to the tune of $25–30 billion a year.[2] A study by The Brookings Institution for the Joint Economic Committee found that federal rules and regulations would cost consumers $102.7 billion in fiscal 1979. That's nearly $500 for every man, woman, and child in the United States. Government regulation is estimated to add $2,000 to the cost of a home, at least $22 to the average hospital bill, and 7 cents to a pound of hamburger.[3] The list goes expensively on.

Besides the astronomical costs of regulation, businessmen complain bitterly about mistakes in and misuse of the information gathered by government agencies. And most of this information is used to exact penalties from the affected corporations and to generate new legislation.

Product recalls, for example, can affect any business, but are probably most visible in the auto industry. In 1977, a record 10.7 million cars were recalled—about as many cars as were produced that year—to repair or replace myriad large and small, new and old automobile ills. The huge costs of these recalls, though difficult to estimate, are inevitably borne by new-car buyers. The definitive study on auto accident causation by a research group at Indiana University found that about 75 percent of all accidents are caused not by mechanical failure but by human failure. That is, speeding, driver inattention, and faulty decision making during crises—let alone the complicating effects of drinking—are the causes of accidents more often than such factors as icy roads, poor road design, or vehicle design and failure (for example, faulty brakes or bald or underinflated tires). Therefore, instead of continuing to press recalls, why not attack the real cause of most accidents through better driver education, regular vehicle inspection, and tougher drinking laws? Unfortunately, the National Highway Traffic Safety Administration found these causes unpopular to support. The agency has chosen instead, because of "political reality," to attack a lesser culprit—Detroit. As E. Patrick McGuire of The Conference Board has said, "The most dangerous component is the consumer, and there's no way to recall him." [4] In short, virtually no one escapes the economic noose of regulatory constraints. And the marginal benefits of even tighter controls in areas like impact-absorbing-bumper and engine-emissions standards cannot easily justify the staggering incremental costs of industry compliance.

Government regulation was once regarded by the public as a necessary protection. Today, despite its many benefits, it has become a cure that may be worse than the disease—a monster that threatens to overwhelm the individual, annihilate the small businessman, and drain big business of most of its potency.

Employee Motivation

To measure the health of the economy, business leaders often keep an eye on statistics for the labor costs per unit of finished product. The recent trends are frightening. Between 1955 and 1965, per unit labor costs rose at a 1.6 percent annual rate; between 1965 and 1975 they rose at a rate of 5 percent; today they are climbing in double digits. The simple fact is that our programs for improving productivity (that is, output per man-hour) are not keeping pace with demands for wage increases.

Unabated, this trend will undoubtedly wreak havoc with our economic system. As workers demand proportionally more wages for less output, profit pressures force prices higher. This in turn produces a new round of even higher wage demands followed by exacerbated price increases. We find ourselves ensnared in the proverbial vicious circle. In short, we are bound to have accelerating rates of inflation if everyone demands more from a fixed or shrinking pie. Improvement of our standard of living is ultimately tied to productivity gains; it is a way for everyone in the system to get a larger piece of the pie—because it increases the size of the pie.

Obviously, one of the fastest ways to reverse these productivity trends is to boost employee motivation. The slack capabilities that exist in our system are incredible, as was demonstrated several years ago when the hourly workers struck Anheuser-Busch, the nation's largest brewer. The company's executives decided to continue operations, manning the breweries with managers. With a workforce that was less than 30 percent of normal, the company produced nearly 80 percent of normal volume!

More recently, Frank Borman, Chairman and President of Eastern Airlines, in an attempt to rescue the company from sagging productivity, soaring fuel costs, and intensified competition brought on by airline deregulation, called upon Eastern's key resource—its employees—to help. He designed an incentive plan that called for all employees to forgo a percentage of their salaries to help ensure that the company netted no less than 2 percent of its gross revenue, the figure required to keep Eastern's many impatient creditors off the company's back. In return for the salary risks, the entire workforce would share the rewards—up to one-third of the profits above 2 percent of revenues. To the amazement of both industry observers and Borman's associates, union management accepted the plan. The outcome? Eastern achieved record net profits for 1978. Increased productivity and better labor-management relations played a large part in the company's financial success, a consequence of employees' willingness to put their own dollars on the line for the health of the entire organization.

Though many corporations continue to experiment with new ways to motivate workers, the trends are not encouraging. The American work ethic seems to be vanishing. By 1976, work hours lost through absenteeism came to 3.5 percent, according to the Bureau of Labor Statistics. Absenteeism costs industry $10 billion a year in sick pay and $5 billion in fringe benefits.[5] Considering the concentration of such problems on Mondays, Fridays, and around holidays, the cost in lost production far exceeds the overall lost time.

Businessmen are justly concerned about the problem of employee productivity. Enormous strides have been made to improve the quality of the work environment. In almost all cases plants are cleaner and safer than they were a decade ago, and jobs require far less physical stress. In addition, workers receive higher pay, profit from more liberal benefits programs, and realize a higher standard of living than previous generations. What is disturbing to business leaders, however, is the belief that the future probably cannot deliver improvements at the same rate as the recent past. Yet workers want even greater gains for reduced job commitment. Something has to give, and the prospects frighten most businessmen.

Technological Innovation

Just as dwindling worker motivation undermines productivity, so technological development—or the lack of it—affects the potency of the nation's productive might. The United States is experiencing a perceptible decline in its rate of technological advancement and an erosion of its once vaunted technological leadership.

Part of the problem is simply that we have reduced the proportion of resources that both government and industry invest in research and development. At the federal level, R&D expenditures represented 3 percent of GNP in 1963; by 1978 it represented only 2.2 percent. Business investment follows a similar pattern.

The absolute decline of R&D funds is only part of the story; the mix of spending has also shifted dramatically. Only 16 percent of industry's R&D budget now goes to support basic research; in 1956, 35 percent of such funds were so invested.[6] Because the decline of expenditures for downstream development has not been as great as that for basic research, the repercussions of this policy shift will become most visible only when the inventory of basic technological breakthroughs is depleted.

The importance of technology to our economy cannot be understated. A Department of Commerce report in 1977 estimated that technological innovation was responsible for 45 percent of the nation's economic growth between 1929 and 1969. In a few areas, such as electronics, we can still look forward to technical developments that will stimulate growth and help improve the quality of our lives. But in most areas of business, technology is not expected to play as large a role in fostering growth as it once did.

Perhaps the most significant factor in the issue of declining technology is the rising influence of foreign innovation. Japan's increasing pivotal role in the electronics industry is perhaps the most visible example, but the same phenomenon is occurring elsewhere. Pharmaceutical research is increasingly being conducted in facilities outside the United States. And many of the innovations in basic industries surface first in foreign countries and later in the United States. West Germany, for example, has developed new energy-efficient processes for manufacturing cement that enable it to sell its products at price-competitive rates in the United States, despite the enormous transportation costs involved. Now it is building cement plants here, using the same advanced technology.

The United States clearly has a technology problem of major proportions. The current situation does not seem to provide enough return to justify a greater investment in technology. Yet do we realize that we are courting long-term disaster if we don't develop new approaches for nurturing innovation? Many factors may contribute to the dismal drama unfolding: government policies, neglect, uncertain business conditions, and myopic management practices. But whichever player is the villain, some major rebuilding of the role of U.S. technological innovation on the stage of global business competition is required.

Consumerist Activity

Business is facing growing pressures from consumers to accept greater and broader responsibility not only for the consequences of how its products are used but also for a broad range of social and environmental issues that are only indirectly related to product performance. For example, it is reported that the general population tends to support the concept of public-interest watchdogs over business, because, quite simply, the public doesn't trust the corporate superstructure. Business's credibility with consumers has never been at a lower ebb. According to a 1979 Louis Harris poll, only 18 percent of Americans have confidence in business leadership. This is down from 55 percent at the beginning of the seventies and down four points from 1978.

Ralph Nader's attack on General Motors in the early 1960s, over what his group saw as the auto industry's lack of concern for safety, legitimized consumerism. Since then, the consumer movement has grown through both government and grassroots support. Today, the movement's major organizations are politically sophisticated and well staffed. They often have a well-defined special-purpose focus (for example, nuclear energy). Consumerists know the issues surrounding their causes, they develop stiff arguments to support their positions, and they establish and use networks of constituency groups effectively to generate maximum support for their programs. Moreover, they know how to exploit the media. In short, they are a force business must take seriously, a need whose time has come.

The key reason for the existence of consumer groups is that the market mechanism apparently does not make business sufficiently responsive to the needs of its consumer constituencies. A single consumer's refusal to purchase what he or she perceives as a faulty product does not necessarily inspire the producer to improve the product's quality, especially if the problem shows up only occasionally. Thus it is not surprising that product liability represents the central focus of the consumer movement, although it has expanded well beyond this domain. Before Nader's raid on GM, there simply was no effective power base for consumers to voice their complaints against corporate actions.

There is ample evidence that consumerism has made corporations much more conscious of the impact business has on all its constituents. Product designs and warranties are developed quite differently than they were just ten years ago. Products are not only safer and more reliable, but they are also recalled more quickly if there is any hint of a problem.

Yet the consumer movement itself does not threaten most businessmen. They know their companies' reputations rest on the quality of the products they produce, and they do everything within reason to ensure that standards are maintained. What frightens them is the danger of consumerism going overboard. When vocal minorities become adept at grabbing and using power, business is less able to serve the "silent majority," which remains its most important constituency. For example, business is now being held responsible for product design, even when the product is used by a consumer in an irresponsible and unintended way. Early in 1979, *Business Week* reported a case in which a woman won a large settlement because the perfume she squirted into a candle flame flared up and burned her face. The producer lost the suit because it had not explicitly warned against such use of its product.[7]

The pressure from consumer groups for greater corporate responsiveness to their demands is bound to intensify. And while the profit motive must be balanced gingerly against consumer interests, most business leaders wonder what, short of state and federal mandates, can provide that balance. In many cases, companies overwrought with external pressures from consumer groups as well as from regulators find it easier to give in to consumer demands—even those that have no basis for support—and simply pass the added costs on to all product users. But this solution is no less irresponsible than one that claims there is no place for consumerists in the business world. Nevertheless, we see such things happening every day. Malpractice insurance, for example, is now a major cause of rising medical costs.

The general public is also concerned about where the consumer movement is headed. According to a 1976 study commissioned by Sentry Insurance, entitled "Consumerism at the Crossroads," the public is strongly behind the movement. But the public feels that both consumerists and businessmen are out of step with real consumer concerns.

The implications of the consumer movement are evident: We are rapidly moving away from the marketplace and product purchasing as the vehicle for evaluating business performance, and instead facing more direct confrontation with special interests. If business is left with the problem of trying to *satisfy* so many diverse groups, will it be able to *please* any of them?

The Financial Scorecard

Strategic issues such as those just discussed have a major impact on our economic success. Few business leaders would quarrel with the assertion that the disappointing rate of business development in the 1970s is directly related to our inability to deal effectively with these issues, much less provide permanent solutions to them. If the stock market is used as an index of sentiment about our rate of economic development, between 1971 and 1978 we slipped by 12 percent.

The crux of our problem, however, is that other countries either don't face the same issues that the United States does, or have learned how to deal with them more effectively than most U.S. businesses. In mid-1979, *The Wall Street Journal* [8] reported the score of overall return (market plus currency changes) of dollars invested in various stock markets between 1971 and 1978:

MARKET	TOTAL RETURN
Japan	+246%
Germany	+122%
Hong Kong	+72%
France	+45%
United States	−12%

As a consequence of our failure to keep pace on an international basis, the capital the United States needs to get back on track and refuel an economic comeback may simply not be available. If that happens, the downhill spiral could accelerate over time, even if, in the meantime, we figure out what it takes to solve our problems.

This shift away from U.S. stocks is occurring, for example, in the investment of our own companies' pension funds! A 1979 survey by Greenwich Research Associates reveals that 19 percent of the 200 largest U.S. companies invest part of their pension assets abroad, and another 15 percent expect to follow this lead in the next year or two. Just two years earlier, the survey showed none of these companies investing in foreign securities and only 2 percent even thinking about it. The same *Wall Street Journal* article reported that less than $1 billion of U.S. private pension money is invested abroad, out of a total of some $300 billion. But the article adds, "At a recent meeting of investment managers in Chicago, it was concluded that more than $20 billion in U.S. pension-fund money may be invested in foreign securities over the next five years." And though some analysts contend that the U.S. market will regain its luster with the passing of the current recession, many others disagree. We may be creating a self-fulfilling prophecy of the cyclical vulnerability—perhaps even the maturation and decline—of our system.

Is Business Doing All It Can?

Are we facing a situation that is both out of control and out of the hands of business leaders? I believe the answer depends on the posture business adopts to deal with these problems. If we extrapolate the business behavior of the 1970s into the 1980s, the answer is probably "yes." But I'd like to make the case that the environment confronting business need not be out of management's control.

During the seventies the leaders of American business were forced to deal with a wide range of significant problems that did not exist a decade ago. There has been a major shift in the issues that occupy top management's attention, and this has created uncertainties about how the emerging problems should be handled. Justifiably perhaps, most managers have proceeded cautiously. As a consequence, business has been on the defensive in most of these new areas. There has been a tendency to react to the consequences of such problems as new government regulation, rather than confronting the causes with offensive programs.

This cautious managerial posture exists in nearly all aspects of corporate strategy today. Conventional corporate wisdom in investment decisions, for example, dictates spending concentrated in businesses where share of market is large, thus achieving competitive advantages from market control. Companies follow the strategy of cutting their losses where they fail the market-share test, strongly supporting their businesses that do, and seeking acquisitions that are already healthy. For the epitome of current corporate philosophy, consider Strategic Business Unit (SBU) investment profiling.

The Strategic Business Unit:
Long-Term Effects on Innovation

If any single technique has become generally accepted by today's corporate executives as a strategic analysis tool, it is the business profiling methodologies first developed by the Boston Consulting Group and General Electric. The procedure is based on the notion that a corporation's profit-making activities can be separated into self-contained organizations called Strategic Business Units. A company's SBUs are usually defined to meet the following conditions: (1) They have an identifiable external customer base that they are serving (that is, profit centers that sell exclusively to other units in the company are not SBUs); (2) there are identifiable competitors also marketing products to these customers; and (3) the unit has organizational control of the fundamental production capabilities and resources needed to provide products to this market. Once the corporation is divided into SBUs, the unit's management takes responsibility for the classic functions necessary to operate a business profitably.

By decentralizing and segmenting business management decisions, corporate responsibilities can be concentrated on such issues as how corporate resources should be allocated among existing SBUs, in which areas it should acquire or start new SBUs, and which SBUs should be phased out. In essence, corporate responsibility is focused on profiling and evaluating businesses, rather than on specific issues of managing any of them.

The heart of corporate management of SBUs is a methodology that assesses the relative strengths of each unit. This is accomplished by developing an "opportunity assessment matrix" in which all the company's SBUs are positioned. Minor variations in the dimensions of this matrix exist, depending on the specific context in which the system is applied; but the essential characteristics are a plot of businesses accessed according to (1) the attractiveness of the *market* in which the SBU competes (measured by the size of the market and its growth potential), and (2) the *position* of the SBU within the market (measured by the SBU's market share). As illustrated in Figure 1, the system enables planners to classify businesses

Figure I. Strategic Business Unit opportunity assessment matrix.

	Low	High
Strong	General Motors (Auto Industry) R. J. Reynolds (Tobacco)	AT&T (Information Transmission) Texas Instruments (Electronics)
Weak	American Motors (Auto Industry) Brown & Williamson (Tobacco)	Exxon (QYX) (Information Transmission) Intel (Electronics)

Market Position

Low   High
Market Attractiveness

into one of four quadrants, depending on the market's attractiveness and the SBUs position. Examples of companies falling in each quadrant are provided in the figure.

The critical feature of the opportunity profiling system is the criteria used to assess business attractiveness. "Star SBUs," which receive top priority for corporate reinvestment, are those that have a market-share domination of a rapidly growing industry (that is, those that fall in the upper right quadrant of Figure 1). On the other hand, "dog SBUs" are those competing in industries where the market is either flat or declining, and the SBU has a weak market-share position. These SBUs are candidates for divestiture or, at a minimum, no major reinvestment. Ralston Purina's decision to sell its ailing Green Thumb Company, a floriculture concern that felt the pinch of an unexpected slowdown in house-plant demand, is a recent example of the demise of dog SBUs.

Strategic Business Units that fall somewhere between these two extremes, having either a weak market share in a rapidly growing market or a strong market share in a declining market, require a cautious posture. General Electric goes as far as dividing its matrix assessment of SBUs into green areas, yellow areas, and red areas.

The SBU investment profiling methodology has won widespread acceptance by corporate leaders. It is both easy to grasp intuitively and, on the surface, logically acceptable. Underlying the methodology, however, are subtle but significant implications for the posture American corporations take toward development. A key assumption in the assessment process is that market share is a critical factor for business attractiveness. Implicitly, the assessments steer the company away from trying to develop innovative strategies for breaking into markets in which it is not yet a factor. Instead, the company concentrates its resources where success has already existed to capitalize even further on those winning ways. If a corporation wants to enter a market, the methodology's implicit recommendation is that the organization buy into it rather than try to penetrate it from scratch. Thus SBU profiling dictates that existing market conditions—not innovative management thinking—is the key determinant of corporate acquisition and divestiture decisions.

As this investment approach has been adopted by more and more companies, its effects are becoming apparent. Divestiture of dog businesses is taking place on a regular basis; General Electric's decision to get out of the computer business is another, and perhaps the most dramatic, example. In addition, today's giants look to acquire small companies with good management and a strong market position; subsequently, the new parent company offers the focused resources and financial backing required to fuel accelerated growth.

As a consequence of this investment philosophy, sales and profits in each industrial sector are becoming concentrated into a smaller number of competitors. This creates the advantage of greater stability in earnings, but it also raises a major management issue: Does investment concentrated on acquired companies that are already successful sufficiently spur innovation in the industry?

Investment in Innovation

Many companies that have been using the SBU opportunity assessment system for some time have begun to see that more and more businesses are drifting out of the green areas into the yellow and red zones of the matrix. Many would argue that this is the inevitable consequence of the economic environment we face today. But is this development outside the control of business? Whose responsibility is it to produce green areas? If we categorically reject innovative investment in areas that the matrix defines as unattractive, are we creating a self-fulfilling prophecy?

The investment rules generated by the opportunity assessment matrix aren't always correct. The athletic shoe market is a classic case. Declining birth rates, leading to a reduced market for children's athletic shoes—a market dominated by Keds—would frighten most companies into perceiving this industry as a red zone of opportunity, unless one were to acquire a market leader. The West German company Adidas had to show American shoemakers that their perception of the size of the market, the products that could be introduced into it, and the prices that could be charged for those products were substantially different from the stable, static, nonglamorous view that previously characterized most assessments. The specialty sports shoe market now represents one of the most rapidly growing, competitive, and profitable consumer products businesses anywhere.

How many more Adidas-like opportunities are we missing? Though that question can never be precisely answered, one thing is certain: The more we concentrate management thinking into philosophies of buying established and successful businesses instead of into philosophies of investing in innovative possibilities, the less likely we are to recognize potential opportunities. If everyone takes the "safe" investment strategy, we will never know what we gave up. In order to reestablish ourselves on the frontier of innovative excellence, we must violate investment rules in which opportunities are judged on existing market conditions. We must look primarily at the potential that innovation can create.

Unfortunately, the managerial mood in American business today is not oriented enough toward bold pioneering in untapped areas. The fight to maintain economic stability during the seventies has created a conservative and protectionist mood among business leaders. In fact, during the late 1970s a number of large companies with excess cash decided that the repurchase of their own stock was the best investment they could make with such funds. This strategy is the ultimate of investment introversion! Under today's pressures, SBU profiling is perhaps the most innovative investment posture one could realistically expect. But it may not be good enough.

Pressures from Outside

Our protective posture may be making us vulnerable to foreign competitors who aren't constrained by our rules. While we are drawing our wagons into a tighter and tighter circle, others, who are not so fearful of risks, are taking chances and succeeding. For the first time in years, American business finds itself fighting a defensive battle to maintain its markets worldwide. Japanese firms are now outselling us in electronics, telecommunications, women's clothing, and other areas in which traditionally the United States has dominated. Gary C. Hufbauer, Deputy Assistant Secretary of the Treasury, succinctly summarized our competitive situation with respect to the Japanese in testimony before a Congressional subcommittee: "Our experience with Japan in the consumer electronics industry—namely, television, radios, audio and trans-receiver equipment—shows some of our weaknesses," he stated. "In 1977, we had a $3.6-billion trade deficit with Japan in high-technology goods, and about two-thirds of this was accounted for by imports of consumer electronic goods." [9]

Japan has become a country we are now forced to respect for its economic prowess. For many years we discounted the

Japanese as "good copiers" of our technology. But such is simply not the case today, as the situation in the auto industry clearly demonstrates. The General Motors R&D department produced the catalytic converter, a mechanism that burns excess hydrocarbons *after* engine combustion. Though this innovation enabled American cars to meet U.S. pollution standards, the Japanese have out-innovated us by introducing the stratified-charge engine, which burns excess hydrocarbons *in* the cylinder, where they add to the engine's power. The result? Most Japanese cars burn regular gas and get substantially better fuel efficiency than their American competitors. As a consequence, Japanese cars continue to increase their share of the U.S. market, in spite of unfavorable currency exchange rates and enormous shipping costs.

American executives are well aware of the economic successes of such countries as Japan and Germany during recent years. Too often, however, we become defensive about their progress. We make the charge of "unfair" competition, because in those countries government and business work in partnership for foreign market penetration. We cite their ability to concentrate on commercial fields because they don't need to support a large defense complex. In short, we place the blame outside our own system.

It's much harder to shift the blame, though, when we look at Sweden's leadership in job enrichment. For ten years American employers have been trying to emulate the job enrichment programs of Sweden's auto manufacturers, particularly the prototype programs developed by Volvo and Saab. Acting under the pressure of severe labor shortages, these firms abandoned the production line and pioneered the team approach to automobile assembly. Teams of workers became responsible for assembling an entire car, according to task allocations they set among themselves. Under the Swedish team approach, management does little more than establish output and quality standards. The actual job structure—that is, the way the assembly workers allocate tasks and responsibilities and integrate themselves into a team—is worked out by the workers themselves, with the help of the supervisor and the industrial engineer. But their activities extend even further; having created entire cars themselves, the workers then become involved in problems of machine design and production, process inspection, and maintenance.

American manufacturers have been experimenting with these Swedish concepts in an attempt to counteract the decline of employee motivation and morale. So far, the efforts have produced only mixed success here, perhaps partly because we are trying to transplant concepts developed in another cultural context. Although a number of companies are examining new approaches to deal with the problem, to date no American approach has captured national attention.

Pressures from Within

External competition isn't the only force that should motivate business to change its present strategies. We don't need to go outside our borders to find situations that ought to be of vital concern to the U.S. business community. Consider the Alaskan oil situation. Everyone agrees on our need for a domestic petroleum source that will free us from the stranglehold of foreign oil producers, especially the Organization of Petroleum Exporting Countries (OPEC) cartel. Yet U.S. oil companies, various levels of government, the transportation industry, and other special-interest groups such as environmentalists simply cannot agree on a plan for the production, distribution, and sale of Alaskan oil. High transportation and operating costs will soon join hands with taxation to push the cost of Alaskan oil production to a level that is totally out of line with what the oil companies—let alone consumers—feel is acceptable. "At this very moment," said *Business Week* in early 1979, "when turbulence in Iran has cut worldwide oil supplies and altered oil distribution patterns, the industry is discovering that the nation's last great domestic oil frontier might simply be too expensive to exploit." [10]

When the system breaks down so badly that we can have an energy crisis while bureaucratic red tape prevents us from capitalizing on an oil source in our own backyard, it's time for some serious soul searching. It's also time to ask our fellow business leaders, are we doing all we can? Is the pressure to minimize risks in the face of large uncertainties so great that we are thwarting innovative solutions to national problems?

Consider how a risk-averse policy creates counterproductive outcomes. As government continues to move into areas of the economy previously dominated by the private sector, the response of business is usually defensive. Through such pressure groups as lobbyists, business resources are channeled to fight the encroachment. Normally, nearly all these resources are spent to expose the weaknesses of the government proposal. Little effort is spent to assess whether the basic purpose of the proposal might be legitimate, and if so, to offer any alternative solutions to the problem that would meet both industry and government objectives more effectively. As a result, government and business invariably approach each other as adversaries.

Let's look, for example, at the recent efforts of national utilities to gain approval for rate increases from the federal government. Such rate requests occur fairly frequently, and the review process is a well-organized ritual. First, the company attempts to inundate the federal investigators with large amounts of data, model analyses, and any other vehicles that can be used to overwhelm them. This tactic seldom works, because the government's rebuttal normally centers on arguing the fallacy of these analyses. The process continues back and forth until one side gets the other into such a corner that there is no escape—which rarely happens—or until they both get tired and reach a compromise solution.

In the case of one utility company, it finally admitted that it couldn't develop a fact-based justification for its requests for a rate increase, because it had no accurate way of estimating the shift in service usage if rates were raised. The federal investigators were already well aware that any assessment of usage was only a guess on the company's part. But the government was no better at forecasting this variable and didn't want to be put on the spot. The "objective" process of assessment had been developed and refined through years of experience; it met some of the needs of each side. Unfortunately, the number of work hours involved in government questioning, company response, more questions, and further response was never estimated. Both sides realized that their efforts meant little in terms of improving the quality of the ultimate decision on the rate increase. Yet both sides felt compelled to act out the charade to the end.

At one point, efforts were initiated to organize a more meaningful basis of cooperative interaction between the parties. This idea was rejected almost immediately by company executives. To reopen the issue, they argued, would make them extremely vulnerable to attack if the investigators chose not to cooperate. Apparently it didn't occur to them that under the existing arrangement they were extremely vulnerable already.

The Bottom Line

It remains to be seen whether business is doing all it can to get itself back on the track. The survival of our economic system could well depend on the business community's commitment to searching for new ways out of old problems and creative approaches to as yet unforeseen problems that the future will inevitably deliver. We simply cannot afford to rely on reactive, risk-averse, often timeworn managerial postures to see us through the bumpy period. Our shock absorbers are wearing out, and the direction in which we're headed is no smoother than the road we've recently traveled. I believe we need to try a different path.

The options we face are not without risk, but alternatives do exist. Consider business's plea for less government regulation. We want government out of business affairs, but what alternatives do we offer to ensure that business will act responsibly? Nothing reinforces the need for government's strong regulatory role more than a company that appears to cover up its shortcomings, rather than take the initiative to correct them, as happened in the recent Firestone fiasco. How much damage was done to the reputation of the business community by Firestone's defensive response to government probes of the Model 500 radial tire? More important, what about the silence from the rest of the business community on the issue? By not taking a stand does business reinforce the public's perception that government regulation is necessary to protect consumer interests? What would happen, one wonders, if industry were to pioneer a self-policing program, instead of waiting for consumerists and government to take the initiative? This is obviously a high-risk strategy, but have any reasonable alternatives to government regulation been offered by business leaders? Can we be against the system that exists without offering viable options? Shouldn't *we* take the initiative to prove that the options we offer can work better than the often outdated methods we currently use?

Opportunities abound for the business community to respond to these challenges with fresh perspectives. Presently consumers are waging an unprecedented backlash against all levels of government, as exemplified by the passage of Proposition 13 in California. Voters are calling for change, literally mandating that government cease some of its activities. What an opportunity for the business community to step forward and show that it can perform some of government's functions better and at less expense! But so far business has failed to seize the initiative.

It is easy, of course, to second-guess business leaders. Theirs is an enormously complex job, because the basic profit responsibilities that are the lifeblood of their existence must be their first concern. But these leaders are paid to set the pace, and solid leadership requires constant reassessment of company priorities. Indeed, the rules of the game are changing rapidly. For years, the oil industry has been more concerned with government efforts to segment companies than they have been with their share of the gasoline market. Management systems must be overhauled to reflect such changes. Executives who yearn for the "good old days" as a way to get back to basics are simply out of touch with today's issues.

A reactive posture to our problems simply won't work. It fosters an adversarial relationship with external groups and puts business on the defensive. The problems we face cannot be avoided; we must confront them head-on. But revitalization will require a new spirit of innovation and risk taking. This, then, is the challenge confronting business today. Our system for creating innovation has changed. If we recognize this fact of life and study precisely how and why the shift has occurred—as is done in the next chapter—perhaps we can anticipate such changes in the future and use them to produce not only happier business executives, but happier consumers and public officials as well.

REFERENCES

1. "That Crusade Against Federal Paperwork Is a Paper Tiger," *Fortune*, November 1976, p. 118.

2. "The Cost of Government Regulation," report on hearings before the Subcommittee on Economic Growth and Stabilization of the Joint Economic Committee of Congress, April 11 and 13, 1978.

3. Weidenbaum, M. L., "Time to Control Runaway Regulation," *Readers Digest*, June 1979, p. 96.

4. "The Mindless Pursuit of Safety," *Fortune*, April 9, 1979, p. 54.

5. "Firms Try Newer Ways to Slash Absenteeism as Carrot and Stick Fail," *The Wall Street Journal*, March 14, 1979, p. 1.

6. "Vanishing Innovation," *Business Week*, July 3, 1978, p. 46.

7. "The Devil in the Product Liability Laws," *Business Week*, February 12, 1979, p. 72.

8. "Assets Abroad: Many Pension Funds Looking Overseas for New Investments," *The Wall Street Journal*, May 24, 1979, p. 1.

9. "Vanishing Innovation," *Business Week*, July 3, 1978, p. 46.

10. "The Great Alaskan Oil Freeze," *Business Week*, February 26, 1979, p. 74.

2
Management Innovation Processes

Success is that old ABC—ability, breaks, and courage.
–CHARLES LUCKMAN

If managers are to solve the key problems that plague our economic system, new approaches are required. The challenge is to develop approaches that will work and implement them. Initially, we need to generate a management process that will foster new ways of thinking about traditional and emerging problems.

Most corporate executives recognize the importance of innovation and constantly encourage their employees to be bold and resourceful in their work. Business leaders know that the corporate commitment to innovation must emanate from the top if it is to take hold. But for all the lip service managers pay to innovation, the pace of business change has not matched the increased turbulence in the environment that business serves. When the chief executive points his finger at senior managers and says, "Let's get more innovation out of our people," the modern corporation does not automatically respond.

I believe that the complex structural and motivational factors present in many corporations make innovation difficult to foster. These factors not only fail to encourage creativity

28

among employees but actually *discourage* it. Thus, before we can look for innovative *solutions* to the problems posed in Chapter 1, we must identify and clear the barricades that keep innovative ideas under, let us say, house arrest.

From Entrepreneur to Professional Manager

In today's corporate environment, the challenge of cultivating innovation differs substantially from what it was only a generation ago. The key to understanding this change is found in the shifts that corporate structure has undergone during that period.

The multibillion-dollar, multibusiness, publicly held, professionally managed corporation has only very recently become the driving force for shaping and pacing the American economy. Until the end of World War II, most business was conducted by organizations that were tiny by today's standards. Usually, each was managed independently by an entrepreneur who started the company and owned all or a majority of it.

The privately held corporation is alive and well; in terms of sheer numbers it remains the predominant form of business organization. Of the roughly one million corporations registered in the United States in 1975, about 980,000 were privately owned family businesses.[1] Nevertheless, the overall influence of the small business on the nation's economy continues to decline. In 1955 the *Fortune* 200 largest industrials accounted for less than 42 percent of total manufacturing sales; by 1977 they accounted for nearly 67 percent.[2]

This shift in the concentration of decision making to large companies over the years has produced a major change in the way we achieve economic advances. In the past, key business decisions were most likely made on an independent basis by the owner-entrepreneur of the organization. Seldom did he have much objective data to justify decisions, and he usually had little or no formal training in the principles of management. As a result, he often made mistakes. If his errors in judgment were too great, his business failed.

There is little doubt that the quality of business decisions today is, on the average, superior to that of the days of the untrained entrepreneur. The chances of a catastrophic failure are substantially less. Better decisions lead to an overall higher level of efficiency and effectiveness in our economic system. And even when a large company gets dangerously off track, as Chrysler has, the chances of going out of business are quite low. But this change also creates new challenges for management. As we implement procedures that reduce the number of poor decisions, we also inevitably make it more difficult for the radical but brilliant solution to be accepted.

Entrepreneurial Era

In the entrepreneurial age of the past, management styles varied widely. Because owner and manager often sat in the same chair, organizational structures and operating techniques tended to reflect the idiosyncrasies of the man running the show. Many company practices lacked common sense, wasted time, and were generally inefficient. But some of them turned out to be brilliant innovations, such as Henry Ford's application of production-line techniques to the manufacture of technologically sophisticated mass-market products. Early entrepreneurs treated management experimentation and innovation as a means of gaining a competitive advantage within an industry. But as successful as Ford's "one model, one color" approach was at the time, the marketing-oriented strategy of product-line diversification initiated by GM's Alfred Sloan soon made Ford's philosophy obsolete. And for each of these spectacular ideas, there were thousands of innovations that didn't survive the test of competition and in the end cost the entrepreneur his business. Moreover, many strategies were successfully developed by one company and gradually adopted by others.

During that early development of modern management principles, entrepreneurs did not actually promote innovation as a separate and discrete activity. Progress simply happened in the natural course of things. It was expected that no two companies would be very similar in the way they were managed. Innovation was not a management objective; rather, it was a natural consequence of the large number of personal management experiments created by differences in style. The philosophy was Darwinian. Companies either adapted to the improvements that others developed or went out of business. Thus, even though the average quality of decision making was relatively low, the overall rate of improvement (what we now call innovation) was extremely high.

Although most of the successful innovations that emerged from this period of economic development have been assimilated into standard business practices, some large companies with strong ties to the business principles of their founders continue to operate in relatively nontraditional modes of management. Three examples concerning employee practices illustrate the types of stylistic individualism that can still produce business success.

FAIR TREATMENT FOR ALL

A well-known, family-held consumer packaged goods company got its start in the 1920s. The owner and chief executive of the company operated with relatively few guiding principles, all of which were well known to all employees. One of these principles was that all employees should be treated on as equal a basis as possible. Many companies would espouse similar philosophies, but few executed them to the extent that this entrepreneur did. Consider some of his policies.

- Elimination of closed offices for everybody, including the CEO.

- Elimination of executive parking privileges; the workers first at the plant in the morning got the best parking spaces.
- Requirement that everyone in the company punch a time clock every day; those who reported on time got a 15 percent bonus.
- Publication of salaries for all positions in the company.

The spirit of equality influenced in many subtle ways the day-to-day handling of personnel situations. No union was ever introduced into any of the company's facilities, and the spirit among employees and their respect for what the company stood for were unusually high. Today, the company remains completely family-held and has an annual sales volume well in excess of a billion dollars on an international basis. Although the feeling for equality of employee treatment remains today and most of these rules continue in practice, there is gradual but increasing pressure from senior managers to revise the operating policies so that they are more "in tune with the times."

PATERNALISM FOR EMPLOYEES

A major family-dominated company in Mexico has done as much to take care of the total welfare of its employees as any company I know. Among the programs that the company has established are:

- A vast social, educational, and recreational complex for employees. This provides not only workers but their families as well with a quality of life outside the company that is significantly better than anything they could obtain unaided.
- A housing acquisition program for employees in which the company subsidizes the building of homes and sells them to employees at cost. Mortgage loans are guaranteed

by the company. By the time the employee retires, he or she owns the home outright.

- Guaranteed income upon retirement, a plan in which the employee is guaranteed that he or she can retire for life, and for a spouse's life, at the salary level enjoyed upon retirement.

- An inflation-protection program upon retirement, in which company stores supply retirees with food and clothing at preinflation prices. Since the institution of this practice in 1946, prices in the stores have not risen.

American executives who have visited this Mexican firm have often asked how the company can afford such employee benefits. The company points to statistics that have been developed on the quality of job applicants, the high rate of employee productivity, the low rate of absenteeism, and the fact that labor is not unionized. With such sound justification to back the plan, company officials answer, "How can we afford *not* to continue these programs?"

EMPLOYEE OWNERSHIP AND DECISION PARTICIPATION

Worldwide industry leadership of one U.S. manufacturing company is based on a unique management philosophy. The company emphasizes cost cutting and rewards exceptional performance with profit sharing through year-end bonuses. This plan raises the average annual earnings of all the company's employees to about double that of its competitors. Yet total employment costs as a percentage of sales are below the average for the industry, while productivity and profits are extremely high. In addition to bonuses, the company offers employees incentives to cut costs while maintaining the level of quality that has established its leadership position. Moreover, the company provides security to its employees by guaranteeing at least 30 hours of work 50 weeks a year after two years of service. The plan is not, however, a one-way street. Workers must be willing to accept transfers and to work overtime when requested. Bonuses are based on a merit rating system—as are promotions—rather than on seniority. There are stock purchase plans, employee representation in management decisions, and a team approach to work organization that gives workers extensive independence in determining work schedules and procedures and considerable responsibility for product quality.

Today's Business Environment

The Darwinian sense of business survival that existed during the entrepreneurial era led logically to concentration of corporate power among continually fewer companies. The organizations that were the first to discover and implement significant new ideas grew in size and power, while the weaklings perished. With each generation of innovation, it is becoming more and more difficult for a newcomer to enter a given industry from scratch and compete on an equal footing with the leaders.

The concentration of power has continued wherever antitrust regulations have permitted it. In the 1920s and 1930s, the consolidation of the auto industry took place. Today, the brewing industry is struggling to lower the number in its ranks, and agriculture continues to move in the same direction. This trend is the natural consequence of economics and competition.

The issue of how a reduction in the number of competitors in an industry affects the quality of products and services is still hotly contested by government and business groups alike. The federal government contends—in theory at least—that fewer competitors undermine consumer footing and thus the entire economy. Hence federal regulations have been enacted to try to stem the rising tide of corporate mergers. The government's deepest concern is that large corporations in different industries are now merging into conglomerates, creating new pockets of both political and economic power. The Justice Department reported recently that 80 mergers took place in 1978, compared with 14 in 1975, with total purchase values of $34.2 billion and $11.8 billion, respectively. Interestingly enough, recent mergers have been almost exclusively of a conglomerate nature, according to the testimony of John H. Shenefield, Assistant Attorney General of the Department's Antitrust Division. This is a trend, he believes, that works against competition; and competition, he says, "provides an irreplaceable spur to efficiency and creates diverse sources of innovation." [3]

Despite the federal government's declared stance of encouraging competition in the private sector, the government's own actions often work at cross-purposes. As government regulations increase on all fronts, companies are finding that their ability to succeed is as much dependent on how closely their operations come to regulatory compliance as on their managerial and strategic acumen. A new product concept that by even conservative estimates ought to "make it big" is only the beginning of getting the product into the market. The ante for complying with all government regulations is becoming too high for anyone not already well established in the industry to make a successful entry. Food and Drug Administration regulations, for example, make it virtually impossible for anyone besides one of the major drug companies to obtain FDA approval for a new drug.

An early 1979 *Wall Street Journal* editorial, entitled "Down with Big Business," gets to the heart of the regulatory issue. The article centered on GM's decision to back President Carter's voluntary wage-price guidelines.

> All this is brought to mind by General Motors' current corporate citizenship campaign. GM is telling us how to lick inflation, "A voluntary program will work, if everyone volunteers." GM Chairman Thomas A. Murphy has written chief executives of the rest of the *Fortune* 500 to urge compliance with President Carter's wage-

price guidelines. And GM has taken out newspaper ads to exhort the populace and brag about its own "commitment" to mother, flag, and the Council on Wage and Price Stability.

Now, this may seem like a strange time to start campaigning for the wage-price control program. It's one thing to board the Titanic as it leaves port, but quite another to come on board when water is coming over the gunwales. In its ads, GM was thoughtful enough to clear up this mystery quickly, etching in boldface the following words: "We have written to our suppliers, informing them of GM's commitment and asking them all to make the same commitment."

So this time, GM and Jimmy Carter are ganging up on the XYZ Bumperlight Lens Company. Five years from now, with the help of Mr. Carter, Mr. Kahn, and so on, XYZ Bumperlight Lens will be the XYZ plant of the lens section of the light division of the bumper arm of the manufacturing subsidiary of guess who?

These insights are gradually helping us to understand why the very biggest businesses are such unreliable allies in the fight to preserve a free-enterprise economy. We're sure, of course, that Mr. Murphy thinks of himself as a capitalist, and can give as stirring an "economic education" speech as anyone around. We're sure that it has never even occurred to him that since GM has a bigger cushion than its suppliers, it can grind them down if the economy is locked up in price standards. We're sure that he and other GM officers have persuaded themselves that the government is waging fiscal and monetary restraint, and sincerely believe that wage-price voluntarism will help it work faster.

For all that, self-interest finds a way to get itself expressed, and the business giants have rather equivocal interests in free enterprise. They always have the option of doing everything lefthanded and backward if that's what the government wants; indeed, that kind of regulation gives them an advantage over less durable competitors. A lot of little guys can make nuisances of themselves if they start resigning from giant research, inventing things, and raising money to form their own companies that compete with the gidget section of the widget division. And GM and du Pont and Exxon and GE are so big even the government has to come to terms with them, or so at least they can believe. And what could be so bad about becoming a public utility and being allowed 8 percent or so on whatever you invest? It works for Ma Bell.

This is of course a caricature of big corporations, their executives, and their motives. But it is a caricature drawn to highlight an impulse that we do think accounts for otherwise inexplicable parts of their attitudes toward free enterprise. Historically, capitalist economies have prospered through competition, innovation, and particularly a sensitive price mechanism transmitting unimaginably efficient signals for less production here and more investment there. If you freeze the system you will lose its thrust toward progress. But in many ways GM's life will be easier. So don't look to big business for unequivocal defenses of capitalism. We guess that's up to the folks at XYZ Bumperlight Lens.[4]

The editorial may have been unfairly critical of General Motors; GM made that point in a letter to the *Journal*'s editor. But whether overstated or not, a basic problem—cultivating innovation in a world dominated by big business and big government—remains. (It is interesting to note that while government does everything it can to reduce the power of big business and create more competition, it systematically eliminates direct competition for its own functions with a claim of "redundance." The federal government is in fact the biggest monopoly of all.)

The complexities of today's economy and the multiplicity of pressures on those who operate within the system make it unlikely that the United States could return to the "Darwinian-entrepreneurial" approach to innovation, even if that were desirable. The challenge must be met from within the corporate structure in order to foster new and different approaches. Let's look at some of the specifics of the problem.

Major Challenges

The replacement of the owner-entrepreneur with the professional manager probably has had greater significance for corporate innovation than any other recent change in the business environment. This development creates some enormous but subtle challenges for senior managers.

The MBA degree, now considered a prerequisite for climbing the corporate ladder, has legitimized management as a profession. The explosion of bright young men and women in pursuit of the MBA over the last ten years demonstrates the corporate demand for the degree. According to the Association of MBA Executives, some 10,000 MBA degrees were awarded in 1968; in 1979 that number soared to over 50,000.

The attractiveness of the MBA has emerged hand in hand with the establishment of generally accepted business practices, applicable to managerial processes in all types of businesses. With the help of the computer, companies now use "canned" software to develop information systems and decision-support models. Software is developed in such a generic sense that its usefulness is minimally dependent on the characteristics of either the company or the industry in which it will be employed. This standardization is the result of the wide acceptance of established management procedures.

One reason for this generalizing of management practices is the mobility of today's manager. Statistics show that 50 percent of the nation's MBAs will leave their first job within two years after graduation. This mobility enables managers to acquire new practices in their subsequent positions and to carry others from former to new employers. Not only do corporations accept such job switching, but many of them encourage it through their promotion and compensation practices. The result of all this is much greater communication within the business community on appropriate and inappropriate ways to handle difficult managerial problems. In addition, business publications, professional meetings, and trade associations are playing an expanded role as vehicles for managers to exchange ideas and information.

The upgrading of the professionalism of management has unquestionably improved the average quality of decisions made in corporations today. But the "group consensus" that is created through these communications channels has also undoubtedly narrowed the range of thinking about alternatives to accepted approaches. Herein lies the danger to innovation. As corporations standardize their management systems, a manager's performance is measured increasingly by how well he uses the generally accepted approach; there is little incentive to look for alternative approaches that deal with problems in fundamentally different fashions and that might produce better solutions. The implicit objective is to avoid disasters by operating on safe ground. Thus, just as the success of many corporations is dependent in large part on the company's compliance with regulatory constraints, managers are implicitly encouraged to perform well within the bounds of convention, rather than to perform innovatively.

This situation creates opportunities for management consultants to recommend new principles that companies should follow in making decisions. Consultants are often the catalysts that trigger a change in management methods. But do they really help build permanent improvements? One of the best known of these consultant groups is the Strategic Planning Institute in Cambridge, Massachusetts, headed by Sidney Schoeffler. SPI has established a confidential data base on more than 1,700 products and services for some 200 companies. Schoeffler analyzes the data associated with product success and failure to develop "strategic rules" that companies ought to follow in managing their businesses. He recently discussed the approach and its results:

> "Feed a computer a set of known characteristics," Schoeffler insists, "and they will account for 80 percent of what causes success or failure. Only 20 percent of what happens to any product is a matter of management skill or luck." More than that, Schoeffler asserts that the laws of business his computer has discovered apply almost uniformly, whether you make cars or candy.
>
> So what are the rules of the game according to Schoeffler's SPI computer? Clearly one of the most important ones is that if you don't already have a major market share for a product, don't try to

build it with research and development spending; chances are it will go down the drain.

Maybe you already figured that out. It does seem reasonable. With a seat at SPI, your printout will demonstrate it clearly not only with a projection of your own company's return on investment, but also with a rundown of comparable efforts already in the data bank of history. Armco Steel Corporation's prefab buildings division was considering some big new-product developments until it plugged into Schoeffler. "Once we perceived clearly," says one Armco executive, "that we were number three or four behind the leader, which had twice the market share of its closest competitor, we junked our innovation plans. If we weren't the leader, we shouldn't be acting as though we were." [5]

I am sure most entrepreneurs would argue rather strongly with Schoeffler about the basis for formulating managerial strategies. But Schoeffler's position is being used in more and more companies today, even if his rules are not. This situation has important consequences for the way progress (innovation) takes place. Instead of following one brilliant maverick who establishes a dramatic new trend, we are now on a path on which progress occurs through small and gradual changes that take place at roughly the same time in all the major companies. Increasingly, progress is evolutionary rather than revolutionary.

The consensus of conventional wisdom concerning appropriate management processes has narrowed considerably the focus of attention of today's executives. By accepting the "rules of the game," managers worry mostly about improving their performance ratings within these confines. And because most companies seem willing to make decisions under the same standards, the entire economic system *seems* to be growing progressively more sophisticated in its decision-making processes. The most sophisticated decision-making methods, however, do not necessarily produce the best solutions in every case; but the momentum toward a more narrowly defined set of management principles is difficult to reverse.

It is no wonder that managers spend little time trying to introduce innovative management procedures. Such proposals are highly vulnerable to attack from proponents of the conventional wisdom—positions that have been refined through years of practice at shooting down the opposition. Radical alternatives stand little chance against such entrenched, often hostile adversaries. Furthermore, if by some chance a proposal for a radically different style of management were to be accepted on a test basis, the career risks for the manager who proposes it would be enormous. The failure of such an experiment would clearly put the proposer out of the mainstream of management thinking, a position from which recovery back into the flock of the conventionally wise would be extremely hazardous. In short, few managers are prepared to rock the boat.

Burton Klein, in his book *Dynamic Economics*, contends that the major new advances almost never emerge from the leading companies in an industry. Even when a large company uncovers a technological breakthrough (for example, the transistor at Bell Labs), the prodigy is usually launched by smaller businesses, often composed of maverick teams of engineers and managers that have left the parent company. Klein offers a host of examples. None of the carriage and buggy-whip makers could create a salable automobile; new companies emerged to dominate each new phase of aircraft and aircraft-engine development; Kodak failed to pioneer the instant camera; Keuffel & Essers slide rule engineers failed to respond competitively to the hand-held calculator; and IBM has lagged behind in adopting many major copier and word-processing innovations. Klein points out that the very process of rationalization and bureaucracy by which a company gains industry leadership, complicated by a preoccupation with statistical productivity—simple coefficients between input and output—tends in the long run to render it less flexible, uninventive, and unproductive. After all, can Ford or General Motors, regardless of its marketing abilities, be expected to jeopardize its plant and equipment with radical changes until other, smaller companies have proved out such new technologies?

As a consequence of such risk aversion, it is very difficult to obtain corporate consensus on adopting a radically different *solution* to a problem even when that solution is developed within a generally accepted framework of decision making. More staggering still is the task of getting agreement to adopt a radically different *philosophy* of decision making.

In most corporations today there are simply too many people who say, "But that's not what we're supposed to do," instead of "That's a good idea, let's try it." Let me illustrate. Upon completion of his MBA, a friend of mine decided to go the "entrepreneur route" and set up a small software company to develop and sell on-line computer programs for managers. While working in his office one weekend, he broke a piece off the typeball for the IBM Selectric typewriter he used on a computer terminal. A new typeball would cost $20, and because finances were tight at the time, instead of buying a new typeball he used his physics background and a little ingenuity to patch up the damaged one. It worked, but his ingenuity didn't stop there. The next week he took the ball with the makeshift repair to a metallurgist to find out if the repair could be made permanent. Both men worked on the problem and succeeded in making the typeball tooth stronger than new. They evaluated the economics of the repair and, to make a long story short, my friend now is the owner of a very successful typeball sales and service business. He succeeded because he capitalized on opportunities instead of succumbing to constraints.

How many corporations would have accepted such a radical shift in their business concepts, even if all the statistics on the magnitude and probability of the opportunity were documented? Can we afford to discard alternatives because they don't fit narrow perceptions of what our businesses are or can be?

Innovation demands a wide-angle perspective of the business–government–scientific communities, for developments in one field often lead to breakthroughs in others. Progress in the drug industry, for example, depends mostly on the results of basic medical research. "Space-age" products and processes—for example, strong, lightweight packaging and building materials, and improved weather-forecasting techniques—derive from the demands of space exploration, be it undersea or outer space. The really top managers are those who recognize and, more important, are able to *implement* ideas that may not fit their corporations' entrenched views of themselves.

Corporate executives must ask themselves whether conventional management wisdom is appropriate. Will convention leave the entire system vulnerable to outsiders who may enter the arena with relative ease using a different set of rules? Are we building for ourselves a specialized economic dinosaur?

The issue of convention versus progression of managerial processes is a vital one for top executives to address. If indeed we are moving toward more constrained but artificially defined decision-making rules, we are forcing ourselves into a classic double bind. The very rules under which business must operate and the standards we employ to solve problems may, in fact, undermine the system those rules and standards were established to promote. We may be missing the opportunity to evaluate the system itself, through tests whose results could lead to the demise—but subsequent betterment—of existing rules and procedures. And yet, the more we follow the rules, the less capable we are of recognizing the dilemma into which we are sliding.

Creating Change

I believe the storm warnings are already out for executives. The gradual evolution of our system from entrepreneurial to professional management has put a great deal more pressure on corporations to consciously induce innovation from within. But as corporate power becomes more concentrated, the tendency toward conventional thinking will accelerate. Thus the responsibilities of those at the top of the organization to ensure that innovation occurs—nay, is encouraged at all costs— becomes all the more intense. The key question becomes one of how we can ensure that innovative ideas get a fair hearing within the management structure.

It is my belief that innovation can occur only when there is a constant, conscious effort to reassess the adequacy of the current process by which decision making takes place. To the extent that the process itself has weaknesses that in turn inhibit innovation, the shortcomings cannot be overcome. Therefore, the starting point for assessing why the innovating thinking of many U.S. corporations has stalled is to systematically examine the general decision-making processes executives use. If bottlenecks can be identified, then top management ought to search for ways to redesign these methods and, indeed, the very principles by which they manage. What are the weaknesses that most inhibit corporate innovation? We'll discuss these pitfalls next.

REFERENCES

1. Hershon, S., "The Problems of Succession in Family Business," Harvard University, DBA thesis, 1975.

2. Shenefield, J. H., Department of Justice testimony before the Senate Committee on the Judiciary concerning conglomerate mergers, March 8, 1979.

3. Ibid.

4. "Down with Big Business," *The Wall Street Journal,* April 18, 1979, p. 24.

5. Berman, P., and S. H. Brown, "Anticonsultant Consultant," *Forbes,* June 25, 1979, p. 78.

3
Bottlenecks to Strategic Innovation

He uses statistics as a drunken man uses lamp-posts— for support rather than illumination. —ANDREW LANG

The structures and decision processes of today's *Fortune* 500 corporations have shifted dramatically from what they were just 25 years ago. One important reason for this change is the enormous growth in size and diversity of the major corporations. The multinational, product-diversified company is a relatively recent phenomenon, and the decision-making mechanisms that sustain such organizations have had to grow in breadth and complexity as a result of these expansions.

Computer-related technologies—hardware, software, and communications networks—represent a second driving force that has significantly changed the modern corporate structure. Whether or not an individual is directly involved in computer processing functions, it is all but certain that his or her job responsibilities would change significantly were corporate computer systems removed. Indeed, the overriding focus of American Telephone & Telegraph Co. and other companies in the telecommunications field is to gear up for substantial increases in the demand for corporate data transmission services. Further development and greater sophistication can thus be anticipated in this area.

45

Although some of the changes in managerial processes have been generated by external factors, such as new computer technologies or sheer growth of large organizations, many have resulted from initiatives taken by business leaders themselves. Although few of these internal changes have been undertaken because of corporate commitments to innovation, several have had a direct impact on the ability of the modern corporation to achieve innovation breakthroughs. Unfortunately, many of these changes have made innovation more difficult. Three areas have been particularly significant:

Investment in Data Banks. It is virtually impossible to calculate how much information has been captured and stored in the memories of corporate computers. However, mounting executive concerns over the security of these systems and the potential threat of sabotage suggest the magnitude of their importance.

Investment in Professional Staff. At one time, staff activities were largely restricted to accounting and financial functions. Today, staff functions dominate the corporate scene, with highly trained professionals offering sophisticated advice and analysis in a wide variety of specialized areas.

Investment in Organizational Structure. Because of the multifaceted, often controversial problems that corporations face in today's business environment, business leaders are paying increasing attention to designing new organizational structures and redefining managerial roles. In complex organizations it is an enormous task for even the most accomplished chief executive to bring all relevant factors and information to bear on a decision, and then to ensure that the actions dictated by the decision are properly coordinated and carried out. To achieve this, managers have been forced to redesign their roles to fit corporate systems; fewer executives now assume independent responsibilities for the total performance of any part of the organization.

Investments in data banks, professional staff, and organizational structure are absolutely necessary for the modern corporation to at least maintain its niche in a hotly competitive environment. The decision to make these investments cannot be questioned. But for all the positive benefits that have resulted from these changes, I believe they have had a serious negative impact on strategic innovation. Let's take a careful look at how and why this deterioration has occurred in each area.

Data: Generate New Options or Close Them Off?

In theory, if managers have access to more data from diverse sources, they should be in a position to generate and examine a greater number of decision options. In practice, however, the situation usually seems to work in reverse: the more data available, the fewer alternatives will be considered.

With the explosion of new computer technology over the last 20 years, managers have been provided ready access to staggering amounts of data. This information capability has been used to create vast networks of decision-support information systems, on which managers depend for the "facts" to justify the decisions they make.

I believe this development has created a false sense of security among managers. They assume that the quality of their decisions is improved because of the vast amount of information they can find to support them. What they do not realize is that the information they receive is filtered drastically, so that most of the bad news is purged. Consequently, managers proceed to implement their strategies with supreme confidence. Only when the strategy fails do they realize that their faith in decisions backed by so-called "fact-based research" may be totally unjustified.

This widely held sense of security came tumbling down abruptly late in 1979, when the venerable Federal Reserve was forced to announce that it had overestimated the nation's

M_1 money supply by $3.7 billion over two successive weeks. The embarrassing mistake, caused by a blundered weekly report by Manufacturers Hanover Trust Co., led to a crumbling of bond prices and yet another jump in interest rates. An occasional informational pratfall like this should remind the leaders of government and business that statistics are not reality; nor should America's undiscriminating devotion to numbers—good, bad, indifferent—obscure the crucial difference between the *accuracy* of numbers and the *validity* of their use in making strategic decisions.

Several other examples illustrate the information-filtering process.

Let's Try That Test Again

In 1973–1974, one of the nation's major food producers—let's call it Premium Food Corporation—faced a crisis. Grain prices were soaring, forcing product prices dramatically higher. Premium's competitors faced similar cost increases, but Premium Food had special problems. Because product quality was a hallmark of the company, it had always been willing to pay more to ensure top-quality ingredients. Escalating grain prices, however, had widened the price gap substantially. To compound the problem, competing firms had generally responded to the 1973–1974 price increases by substituting lower quality ingredients wherever they felt it would not have an overly negative effect on product taste. Premium Food faced a major strategic hurdle: Was it willing to reduce product quality in order to ensure price competition.

The company launched a series of tests to determine the extent to which consumers could distinguish product differences resulting from extra care in ingredient selection and processing techniques. The first test results showed remarkably little consumer perception of quality variation. Had there been no vested interest in the outcome for Premium Food, these results would undoubtedly have dictated a strategy shift to lower-quality ingredients.

Because product quality was so fundamental a tenet in Premium Food's management philosophy, its senior executives felt committed to continue the high-standards strategy if there were any way to justify it. Accordingly, the executives questioned the validity of the method used to determine consumer preferences in the product tests. The method—one traditionally used in taste-test research—involved consumer sampling of small quantities of unidentified products under controlled conditions in a laboratory setting. Premium's executives questioned the results on the basis that the tests did not replicate the natural environment in which in-home use would normally take place. Consequently, new tests were designed and executed.

The second test used unmarked product samples delivered to a consumer's home and used on a regular basis over a period of several weeks. These consumer product evaluations were more expensive than the earlier laboratory methods, but Premium's management was less concerned with cost than with the policy implications of the test's results. The redesigned tests produced dramatically different results. They confirmed the importance of quality to a substantial segment of the market. These results provided the company with the data it needed to continue the quality-oriented strategy.

The message should be obvious: Energies expended on data collection are greatly dependent on the beliefs of the decision makers before the work is initiated. Premium Food was willing to spend much more on methods that would confirm predispositions than on methods that might negate them. This aspect of decision making naturally has a great effect on the type of information that even enters the executive pipeline. Let's now take a look at a related but more extreme case.

To Pop Up or Not to Pop Up

Companies that are willing to validate a preferred strategy through data collection methods, as the Premium Food case illustrates, can also readily use data to rationalize discarding one strategy for another. If the market posture of a product is not clearly defined, management can easily drift between extreme positions, justifying each change by "objective" data.

For example, a major competitor of Kimberly Clark (we'll call it Poptional Plus) tried for years to develop a pop-up package for facial tissue that would rival the patent-protected Kleenex box. Finally, Poptional's packaging engineers developed a technique that would approximate the Kimberly Clark feature. Poptional initiated consumer research to test which package consumers favored, although most of its executives were already quite convinced that the pop-up feature was preferred. Sure enough, research confirmed management's prior belief.

The packaging change was made. Almost immediately, the company began to receive letters from consumers complaining about the new feature. Many people liked the fact that the old package permitted multiple tissues to be taken from the box by the handful. A person could thus easily take a dozen or so tissues for travel and use them one at a time. The new package design made this impossible. Consequently, sales eroded for a short period after the introduction. In the long run, however, the new box seemed to have little impact, positively or negatively, on the growth trend of Poptional's product.

About five years after the introduction of the new feature, Poptional Plus suffered a period of shrinking profit margins. Industrial engineers, examining every area in which cost savings might be effectuated, discovered that the pop-up tissue box was costing the company an extra several hundred thousand dollars a year to produce over the old box. Naturally, the engineers wondered whether the feature was needed. Be-

cause of its commitment to cost reduction, Poptional conducted new market research to examine whether consumers
really did prefer this feature. Not surprisingly, Poptional's assessment of the test's results was that they did not. The pop-up
feature was removed. As one might have guessed, customers
unleashed an avalanche of new letters of protest; such
strategic schizophrenia is difficult to overlook. Sales again
nosed down in the short run but gradually recovered to their
original trend level. The pop-up tissue feature may have had
little consequence for the company's overall market position,
but it clearly did nothing to help the development of a viable
strategy with long-term significance.

Here again we find that data collection and analysis—as
highly touted as it is—need not be "textbook neutral" in
order to find universal acceptance in today's sophisticated
decision-making networks.

The Forest and the Trees

Finally, data can become so obstructive that executives lose
sight of the major issues. Such a situation caused near disaster
for the member companies of a major trade association. The
association—let's call it "Associates Anonymous"—had spent
most of its energy over a five-year period fighting proposed
legislation that its members considered economically disastrous to the industry. By selecting and refining data that supported the industry's position, Associates Anonymous gradually developed a very persuasive argument against the legislation.

Unfortunately, Associates was so committed to its position
that it never reexamined any of the basic assumptions that
justified its strategies during the five-year period. In fact, some
fundamental changes had taken place in the industry's cost
structure. Over time, the proposed legislation had become
compatible with changes the members of Associates should
have been making all along in their own self-interest. But

Associates had been so busy fighting the legislation with facts it obtained selectively that it never assessed all the environmental changes on a detached, objective basis. Consequently, changes that were in the best interest of both government and industry were delayed until very late, when Associates Anonymous finally realized that the loss it was suffering could have been avoided.

Implications

As these examples illustrate, statistics can be found to support any reasonable position. Obviously, if one has ready access to a variety of potentially relevant information, the judgmental decisions—which information will be used and how—can defend or destroy an argument. Since data assessments of strategy options normally are conducted by planning staff groups, any commitment to strengthen strategic information systems implies more potential power for the staff.

Is this power used objectively? Do staff analyses provide a balanced evaluation of the strengths and weaknesses of particular strategy options? These questions have been studied in the execution of scientific research, in which judgmental decisions that can bias results are considerably more controlled than in the typical corporate strategy assessment process. In his classic study of the issue of biased staff analysis, the noted psychologist Robert Rosenthal developed detailed instructions on the proper execution of a research program. He then presented the instructions to a group of experimenters with an explanation of the results he expected to find when the tests were conducted. Unknown to the group, Rosenthal gave the identical instructions to a second group of experimenters but with a set of polar expectations. Rosenthal then analyzed the data classified by the experimenters and found that each group had obtained results that tended to confirm the expectations he had given them.[1]

Staff groups simply cannot avoid making judgments in the

process of assessing strategic alternatives. Some of these judgments are made consciously and thus can be reexamined for bias, but most are so subtle that they are not even recognized. The objectivity of staff perceptions deteriorates in making these judgments, which customarily are slanted to please an influential superior. They tend to make the case for a solution known to be preferred by Mr. Big. Even the most conscientious managers—those with a deep commitment to objective analysis—are invariably more pleased when favorable results emerge. Staff members subconsciously respond to this, and a manager who has the reputation for firing the guy who brings in the bad news can accentuate the bias problem.

If bias is severe, subsequent actions can be disastrous. Senior managers formulate tentative options, expecting the assessments of staff analysts to shake out strengths and weaknesses. What they usually receive, however, are confirmations of their own perspectives. Unknowingly, and contrary to even their best intentions, these managers are using a "seat of the pants" management style, but the positive feedback they receive from staff increases their confidence in their own intuitions. As a result they become less willing to listen to proposals from others. As this occurs, innovation wanes. Subordinates become passive and execute only what and when they are told. Even where the assessment process is not overly biased, uncertainty can result. And the problem is becoming increasingly prevalent. The expanding size of corporate data banks and the growing variety of analytic models for using the data bury an ever-increasing number of judgments in the assessment process.

Staff: Supplement to or Substitute for Management?

A second problem that affects the ability of corporations to adopt new innovations is the role of the staff itself. Staff work has been a critical part of executive decision making for many years, but the role of staff has been shifting over time with the development of new techniques in the decision process. The role has become especially critical with the emergence of the "model-building approach," a method of decision making that appeared shortly after World War II.

A model is a simplified representation of reality that can be manipulated to forecast the effects of a specific action. A model need not be formal and precise; it can be a simple, mental framework that is used to analyze a problem and choose a solution.

Today, the purposes and structures of models vary considerably from what they were 20 years ago. There is no question that developments in computer technology have contributed in a major way to the evolution of managerial models, but the basic philosophy of modeling managerial processes has also undergone a dramatic change. The change has been especially significant as it relates to the roles management and staff play. To better understand this change, let's examine the three key phases of model development, each of which has assumed a fundamentally different role for management and staff.

Pre-1960: Experience-Based Management

Until the late 1950s, the quality of managerial decisions depended almost entirely on the experience and capabilities of key decision makers. Before that time, the staff support function for top executives was practically nonexistent. Intuition, not numbers or staff analyses, was critical to effective corporate decisions.

All this began to change in the fifties. Dissatisfaction with the quality of decisions was not the primary reason. Rather, the post–World War II business boom created large new growth opportunities, particularly in consumer goods, which resulted in tremendous pressure to find managers capable of handling the challenges. The additional proven managerial talent simply did not exist, and the time required to provide the experience to new managers was excessive. New vehicles to fill this need were sought. This demand for talented managers to exploit expanding market opportunities gave birth to the era of modeling and the growth of professionally trained staff groups.

The 1960s: Model-Optimized Management

The search for more efficient management techniques led to the emergence of industrial operations research (OR) in the 1950s. Staff groups trained in this discipline were the first to formalize modeling procedures as the foundation for managerial decision making.

Operations research models were originally used to solve military problems, and their development and refinement for industrial applications were well under way in the early fifties. As OR models became accepted and the industrial demand for high-level OR staffs grew, the process of decision making rapidly shifted from a subjective and intuitive focus to one designed to be objective and analytic. Mathematical models were developed to provide the "optimum solution" to managerial problems. Under the new format, it was assumed that the model provided "good" answers to "bad" problems. This philosophy of optimization assumed implicitly that all the major complexities of a problem could be subsumed within the model. The implication of this concept was that the model-building staff would develop solutions to problems, and the manager's role would be to execute the solution generated by the model.

Because OR was a new discipline and thus not well understood by many of the managers employing it, the initial decision-making power granted to many corporate OR staffs far exceeded their capabilities to design and apply valid models to the problems presented to them. However, confident that they could do no worse than the intuitive decision makers of the past, these early modelers seized every opportunity to expand their influence in the decision-making process and took on most, if not all, assignments.

In retrospect, many of the so-called "objective" models produced by OR showed far worse performance than the subjective managerial judgments used previously. Many times, however, the weaknesses of these optimization models were not revealed until after the models had been implemented and had failed. Through costly experience, managers discovered that the reliability of this new generation of decision models was wholly dependent on the validity and certainty of the assumptions upon which each model was built. If the assumptions were not true, the rigor of the approach would be merely a facade.

A well-deserved managerial backlash to the model-optimized decision process led to dismemberment of many high-level corporate OR groups in the late 1960s and early 1970s. The widespread disillusionment with the optimization approach is exemplified by a sign emblazoned on the wall of one high-level corporate manager's office: "I'd rather be approimately right than exactly wrong."

The 1970s: Interactive Management

The reaction to the problems created by the model-optimized decision processes has led to the current trend toward interactive models. These models have been developed partly to capitalize on the advanced technology of on-line interactive computer terminals, and are constructed to give managers the ability to participate in designing the models they use. By plugging into a computer, a manager is able to work with staff groups to insert his or her own assumptions about key problem characteristics. When management alters assumptions statements, staff specialists conduct new model runs. Thus, instead of a single "optimum" result based on a model designed entirely by staff groups, managers can analyze a range of results under a variety of plausible conditions. This arrangement provides solutions that can be judged by managers on a number of criteria—including the risk, robustness, and expected performance of alternative actions—before committing to a final choice.

While the growth of on-line computer technology has stimulated interest in interactive models, most high-level managers remain cautious about how much this trend will improve the quality of decision making. Their concerns are well founded, because interactive models do not resolve the fundamental problem of the role of the staff group in corporate decision making. Many of the most critical assumptions needed to establish a model's basic design are still made by staff analysts, whose efforts define the fundamental structure of the problem. In many cases, the assumptions that managers control are really second-order effects.

The Staff Dilemma

The past 20-year period has witnessed major corporate commitments to upgrade and enlarge staff functions. From some of these endeavors, entirely new disciplines, such as operations research itself, have emerged. But the credentials and scope of virtually all established staff functions—such as legal, tax, personnel, and public relations—have also been enriched and expanded at the same time.

Although corporations have obviously benefited from the improved quality of advice these enlarged groups have provided, the benefits have been somewhat less than corporate leaders might have expected. The key reason for this frustration is that the fundamental roles of management and staff have never been properly clarified. Staff groups normally serve an advisory function, while ultimate decision-making authority and responsibility rests with management. But the boundaries between the two functions are often fuzzy and can create significant organizational problems which hamper decision-making effectiveness.

Corporate planning is a classic example of this problem.

Many companies have created large staffs of professionally trained planners to help wrestle with the complex issues involved in making strategic decisions. Often these staff groups are responsible for actually creating the corporate plan. But when the time comes for the staff to translate the ideas contained in its plan into action programs that the corporation's managers will implement, the exchange frequently breaks down. The corporate plan and the staff analyses that support it become sophisticated window dressings, ignored by managers as they contend with day-to-day operational problems.

Under such conditions, better results might be obtained by eliminating the planning staff altogether and forcing managers to develop their own plans for long-range development, with the expectation that they would be more likely to "deliver the goods" on their own proposals. A plan comprising the ideas of managers, executives believe, may not be as rich as the staff-developed version, but the ultimate rewards for the invested effort would probably be greater. Indeed, such a solution to the nonalignment of managerial and staff roles is consistent with much of the published literature diagnosing the factors most critical to the success of the long-range-planning effort; that is, active participation by managers is often found to be critical to successful planning (see, for example, the articles by Caldwell [2], Lucado [3], and Steiner and Schollhammer [4] listed at the end of the chapter).

Apparently, then, active staff support of managers throughout the planning process is not advisable. Right? *Wrong!*

The real need is not to eliminate staff groups but to clarify the roles managers and staff ought to serve within the corporate structure. The problems of clarifying such roles can best be understood by analyzing the actual working styles of corporate executives. Henry Mintzberg, who has done extensive research in this area, shows that little top executive time is actually spent making decisions in the classic sense. Instead, nearly two-thirds of that time is spent as an information filter of "fresh news" that may be relevant to the organization's strategies. The higher the manager's position in the organization, the more likely that his or her information is obtained from sources outside the company, such as trade associations, government, and unions. This means that a single executive is often the only corporate link between raw information and the company's response to it. Thus the adequacy of a manager's personal filtering network for differentiating relevant from irrelevant information may be the difference between appropriate or inappropriate action and inaction on a major decision. In other words, the quality of the actual decision may be less important than the recognition that a decision is needed.

The information-filter role may be the most important one the executive plays. The approval of proposed actions in response to the information probably commands less overall impact than does the fact that some action was initiated at all. Recognizing the importance of the information-filter role is key to understanding interface problems between managers and their staff groups. Later, we will see that the way a manager "programs" his or her filter is key to the amount of innovation he or she fosters.

The role top managers play as information filters helps explain why staff groups have difficulties providing support systems for managers. The vantage point from the plateau staff members occupy simply doesn't allow them to be party to the vital information exchanges that characterize the executive function; hence, staff analyses are based on a narrower view of company problems than management has. Further, staff analysis systems can be updated only after the manager uncovers an unexpected data source, meaning that the staff analysis is usually created after the fact—like locking the barn door after the horse has been stolen. These conditions nearly guarantee that technical analysis of problems by staff groups will involve extrapolations and approximations to fit emerging conditions—in short, advising the company to proceed with what it is already doing. For example, staff analysis of the consequences of government-imposed wage-price controls does relatively little good after they have been imposed. Strategies for dealing with such an event must be developed prior to implementation of the controls and after management believes they are a real possibility.

This situation suggests the need for a coordinated partnership between management and staff. Each group needs the other. Managers are usually overloaded serving their information-filter function; they have neither the time nor the technical expertise to conduct reasoned analysis of every potential issue. Staff groups, on the other hand, can take the time to develop efficient, effective, and flexible analysis systems within their domain, but they cannot provide instant and categorical answers to new problems that do not fit neatly into their analytical structures. To be at all effective, staff groups need timely, accurate, and complete—that is, unfiltered—information from managers.

Unfortunately, the partnership usually doesn't work very well. In a hurry to act on a hot issue, managers will often choose not to "waste the time" getting staff groups involved. Instead, "quick and dirty analysis" will be done by one or two individuals who already have some understanding of the issues involved. Technical expertise becomes secondary. This results in staff groups becoming even further removed from what's happening in the company, their analytic systems become more outdated, and they are labeled as "ivory tower." When this alienation of staff occurs, managers become even less willing to interact with staff groups, even on issues where time constraints don't exist. As this happens, staff group members often see the handwriting on the wall and either switch careers to the "managerial track" or stay where they are and delude themselves into believing they are "doing their own thing"—which they can do with impunity, since no one is paying any attention to their performance.

The net result is a major collapse in the potential creative synergies that are possible with an effective management–staff partnership. The relationship of the two groups develops into an ever-widening chasm, and creates a system that makes real innovation more and more difficult to achieve.

Organizational Structure: Effective Decisions or Political Actions?

The complexities of today's business environment demand more sophisticated organizational structures. Very few top management decisions can be based on the information at the fingertips of one executive. Moreover, there are vast complexities in assembling relevant information and integrating it into a coherent perspective on a given problem. In response to this problem, new systems of organization—for example, matrix management—are replacing the traditional forms of management, such as product or functional organizational designs.

Accompanying changes in organizational design, companies in all realms of business have undertaken to become more specific regarding job performance. Vague corporate expectations from individual managers—"Help us make a profit" or "You take care of production scheduling"—are no longer sufficient for telling an individual how he or she is expected to relate within the corporate environment.

Clarifying and quantifying criteria for evaluating job performance is a double-edged sword. If the standards are very well designed, the individual can operate within them with the confidence that meeting the defined objectives will both accelerate his or her own career and improve the performance of the organization. But if standards contain defects or are applicable only in certain situations, the individual faces the supreme dilemma: Should you operate within the job parameters you have been given, or violate them to take the actions you believe are right?

With the growing popularity of quantitative job performance

systems, such as management by objectives (MBO), managers are less inclined to challenge the relevance of the criteria upon which they are judged. This places a major responsibility upon those who establish the criteria to be sure the standards are appropriate. In many cases they may not be, and this problem is one more factor that thwarts innovation.

Another major problem with quantitative job evaluations is that they rely on criteria that can be measured, but not necessarily those that are most relevant. This induces managers to take actions that shield them on the most visible—and often the most vulnerable—aspects of their jobs.

Consider the following situation. A marketing manager is faced with a pricing decision for a product that competes in a price-sensitive category. His competition has reduced prices, and the manager must decide whether to follow with a price cut or to hold the line. Assuming the decision is to be driven by profit considerations, the critical issue is easy to define: Will the company realize greater overall profits if it maintains the higher price and makes a higher profit margin on reduced sales or, alternatively, if it reduces prices and makes a lower profit margin on increased sales volume? There is, however, another factor to be considered—the evaluation of the manager. If the manager maintains the high price and is wrong, the error is highly visible and measurable because of the lost sales. But if he or she cuts the price, it is nearly impossible to prove the decision was wrong, because no one can accurately estimate the sales loss that would have occurred if the price had not been reduced.

The pressure to cover oneself against visible mistakes is great, and most managers understand and utilize such a shield very well. They play the game within the defined rules, especially in areas of high risk. For example, if a new venture idea does not seem to be progressing, the safest solution is to simply abandon the effort. On the other hand, selling the project to another company or turning it over to entrepreneurs in-

terested in continuing its development on their own creates
visible risks; if the project eventually succeeds under different
management, such a turnaround is a bad reflection on the
managers who couldn't bring it off.

The same pressure to avoid visible risk makes managers
reluctant to take the initiative to prevent emerging problems.
Usually a corporation has the widest variety of options available to it if it acts offensively before the problem is highly
visible, rather than defensively after it is apparent. But unless
prevention is clearly the manager's intention, he will be inclined to react to, not initiate, action. His reasons seem rational enough. The consequences of successful early preven-
tive action are never seen because the action prevents the
problem from ever occurring. But if early action is taken and it
fails, the individual could easily be blamed for creating the
problem. Thus, faced with the alternatives either of initiating
action in an environment that is superficially nonthreatening
in order to maintain the status quo or of waiting until the
environment demands a response, most managers choose to
wait rather than to risk a blemish on their records. Such behavior, of course, is the antithesis of the innovative spirit
needed to solve many of the problems we are facing.

Executives continue to struggle with the design of processes
that will encourage more innovative strategies. The three
areas we've just reviewed—use of data, staff roles, and organizational pressures—can, if treated appropriately, help in several ways, and I'll discuss these shortly. Meanwhile, we'll
examine ways in which many companies are using management committees to spur innovation.

Strategy Committees: A Healthy Sign, But No Panacea

More and more companies are recognizing that traditional
management principles are just not meeting the challenges of

today's turbulent environment. One widespread response to dated methods is the concept of Strategic Committees. The intent of such committee mechanisms as the Office of the President is to bring the diverse perspectives of managers together without following the normal chain of command, in order to develop fresh, energetic strategies. The assumption underlying this tactic is that through direct interaction and shared responsibility for designing and implementing corporate strategies, the executives on the Committee will find a way to integrate their perspectives into plans that deal with the organization as a system rather than as a set of independent parts.

This is a very positive stride. It offers the possibility of breaking down traditional thinking about problems and solutions into a new synthesis that can be applied holistically to corporate management. Let's look at some of the possibilities that can be created through such systems integration.

Consumerist Problems Solved by Personnel

Because of the compartmentalized thinking that is characteristic of rigid organizational structures, we normally expect that the "group facing the problem" is in the best position to solve it. Thus the typical corporate response to pressures from consumer groups is to assign the company's public relations department or an equivalently mandated group to deal with the problem. But while the company's PR spokesmen may not be the most effective ones to respond to the problem, the Strategic Committee may be able to figure out who is.

Consider the following situation. A consumer products company recently conducted a survey to learn more about the consumerists who were supporting a particular issue. The survey's findings showed that the typical consumerist was a white, middle-aged, well-educated suburban housewife whose children were all in school. She was bored with her role in life, and she spent her energies trying to help institute positive social changes. There was one further piece of significant information: Many of these women had sought meaningful work within the corporate structure and had either been turned down or been asked to take a typing test. The message should be clear: If the corporation insisted on divorcing its consumerist strategy from its employee career development strategy, it would pass up some highly attractive solutions to both challenges.

Consumerist Problems Solved through Marketing

Can corporations' social and profit responsibilities be managed as one issue? These seemingly incompatible bedfellows are assuming startling companionship in a number of organizations on a small-scale basis. Their strategy is quite straightforward: Pledge a portion of profits from branded products to support specific social causes. Then advocates of the social causes can directly support them through the purchases they make as consumers. This strategy appears to work best for products that have functionally equivalent brands, such as soap, coffee, or razor blades, but a modified version has also been used with big-ticket items. Datsun offered to plant a tree for any person who took a test drive, an obvious appeal to environmentalists. A direct-purchase strategy was used by Bristol-Myers when profits from some of its toiletry products were used to support New York high school athletic programs during the city's fiscal crisis. A regional beer has quietly supported the gay liberation cause in California and is said to dominate other brand sales in gay bars. The success of strategies designed to support profit and social responsibilities simultaneously requires that the issues be analyzed together, rather than as separate objectives for the corporation to meet.

Pension Funds and Career Planning: One Problem

Consider another case in which two apparently different problems are really elements of the same issue. Within the past five years, business has seen the federal government take two giant steps in the regulation of corporate personnel policies. In 1974 the Employee Retirement Income Security Act (ERISA) was passed, and in 1978 mandatory retirement prior to age 70 was outlawed for most employees. The constraints imposed on corporate personnel policies by these changes have raised a number of concerns among businessmen.

With respect to ERISA, the concerns center on pension liabilities. Specifically, businessmen are concerned because (1) as of 1978, corporate liability for unfunded pension benefits involved up to 30 percent of corporate net worth in addition to pension fund assets; and (2) through the Pension Benefit Guaranty Corporation, businesses have financial responsibility for unfunded pension benefits of all other ERISA participants. Thus, if a business downturn caused weak companies to fail—thereby spreading their pension liabilities over a narrower base—other companies could be affected.

Concern over mandatory retirement focuses on criteria for evaluating job performance, particularly in white-collar occupations. Because the legislation has only recently been enacted, companies are concerned about the mechanism that will have to be established to administer the new law. Several unresolved questions remain, however. What is acceptable as an objective test for competency? How can career paths be planned for younger employees in view of uncertainty over retirement of older employees? How active will government regulators become in corporate personnel assessment procedures?

Most corporations have treated problems related to ERISA and mandatory retirement separately, because the former relates to actuarial and investment issues, whereas the latter relates to personnel issues. But the two concerns are really the head and tail of the same problem, that is, the transition from full-time work to retirement. To the extent that employees work past normal retirement age, the pressure on pension funds can be diminished. Furthermore, as pension vesting occurs at an earlier age and with fewer constraints, flexibility in job changes and/or early retirement increases for both the employee and the employer.

Many of the issues of employee motivation and productivity might be addressed by capitalizing on complementary corporate and personal needs. Such alternatives as permanent part-time work and second career might become more widespread under a new approach to the problems. The dark clouds of both ERISA and mandatory retirement could begin to dissipate if they are considered together as part of a total system redesign. But this enlightenment requires the broad view of groups such as Strategy Committees to perceive such a vision.

The Fly in the Ointment

Though there are obvious advantages of an integrated approach to corporate problems through vehicles such as the Strategy Committee, the many companies that have instituted them have discovered that merely creating such a group does not guarantee positive results. The Strategy Committee format normally falls far short of providing the intended benefits of problem integration, and in many cases it actually results in worse decisions. The approach usually succeeds in one important sense: divergent perspectives of the committee's members will surface, which helps the group understand the types of strategies each member supports or rejects. Preferences also surface in both the philosophy of management (the aggressive radical versus the conservative tried-and-true advocate) and the loyalty to a functional or business base (marketing versus production orientation, or new business development versus protecting the profit base).

Getting divergent views out on the table is fundamental to the success of group decision processes. Perspectives that make sense from a department or division viewpoint aren't necessarily correct when analyzed from an overall corporate stance. Actions that optimize the performance of the parts of a corporation do not usually result in the best overall performance for the system. To assume otherwise is like trying to design the best car by having different engineers independently build the best carburetor, transmission, brake system, and so on, and then assembling the pieces. The Strategy Committee is a vehicle for identifying parochial interests so that integrated designs can be developed from an overall perspective.

When companies establish committees to formulate corporate strategies, the major problem usually occurs when the group tries to integrate the ideas from the participants. The result is something less than a powerful, synthesized, robust corporate strategy—one that rests on a reasoned and objective assessment of the divergent positions the participants represent. More often, committee members polarize on major issues. The advocates of the various strategy options assemble an arsenal of statistics and arguments and are met with counterarguments based on new data or reinterpretation of existing statistics to offset the strength of the opposition.

This argument/counterargument harangue inevitably causes the deterioration of decision-making performance, because a synthesis of positions becomes almost impossible to identify. Ego investments in each opposing position become more and more deeply implanted. Often, factions surface during the process, and no decision is ever taken on the issue. Either the concerns build to a crisis, in which action is taken by brute force, or they diminish to the point that management must turn its attention to other, less heated issues rather than continue in political turmoil. If a decision *must* be made, the strategy is often forged through political compromise. Positions held by the polarized executive forces are woven into a strategy that has few common threads and little likelihood of succeeding. I speak from sad but vivid firsthand experience on this point. Consider two examples of past clients' problems.

CONVENIENCE-ORIENTED FOR WHOM?

Bon Appetit (not its real name) is a major food and beverage manufacturer. It prides itself on having sophisticated production technology that keeps costs low, but it has never possessed exceptional marketing strength. One of the company's main food products requires relatively long preparation time. In response, a competitor introduced a new product that was an "instant" version of the traditional form. Not only did the new product reduce preparation time and effort, but it was easier to carry, because it came in a foil package instead of a can. The new use and added convenience of the instant form made it a success.

Bon Appetit had to react. Its R&D staff quickly developed an instant form of the product that it felt was superior to its competitor's. However, the production staff was less enthusiastic about the new product, because the equipment and production technology were completely new to them. Grudgingly, production finally went along with the new instant formula.

But the stickiest disagreement developed over how the product would be packaged. The production people wanted to put it in a can, even though this significantly reduced the convenience of the product. They argued that the overall product quality would be higher if it were packaged in a can. Production won this round of the product design. The final result was a strategy best described as "instant product convenience in an inconvenient can." The product failed in the market.

STRATEGY RATIONALIZATION

In the late 1960s, a $200-million company decided to undertake a diversification program. An executive planning committee was established, consisting of the president and vice-presidents, to oversee the expansion effort. The executive vice-president assumed responsibility for the acquisition strategy.

The first task of the planning committee was to determine criteria for acceptable acquisitions. The group tried to define the boundaries of the company's current businesses, but could not agree on any operationally feasible definitions. After several months of spending time without making progress, attention shifted to a different issue: What types of acquisitions would have the greatest synergy with existing businesses? Again, the committee's efforts produced no agreements.

Out of frustration, the executive vice-president started to move; he began acquiring companies without a strategy. Since the early acquisitions added profit and growth, his business judgment appeared sound. Because of his success, the executive planning committee worried less about criteria for new acquisitions. Instead, they spent their time trying to develop a rational explanation for the business complex that already existed—an activity they deemed essential, since they did not want to be considered a conglomerate. Each new acquisition made the task more difficult, but it seemed to be a problem the committee enjoyed trying to solve. The fact that the rationalization efforts had no significance for future business development seemed to be of little concern to committee members. They were at least able to work together on this problem.

Unfortunately, the happy times ended abruptly in the early 1970s. The economy turned down, and the performance of many of the acquisitions dropped significantly. On top of that, the hot hand of the executive vice-president turned cold. He began buying companies that almost immediately soured. As a result, the executive vice-president was fired, the executive planning committee was disbanded, and "growth strategy" became a politically unpopular term around the office. The company failed to understand that committing resources to develop a growth strategy is not the same thing as developing one. Executives blamed the concept of such a strategy for their problems, whereas its execution by the planning committee was the real cause of its demise.

The Key Problem with Committee Decisions

For committee decision processes to work, there must be a mechanism to integrate diverse perspectives. As efforts to evaluate alternatives accumulate, while those of integrating perspectives decline, the process becomes competitive. To be successful, the group decision processes must explain *why* different strategy options have been formulated. Most strategy alternatives are produced by differences in fundamental assumptions about the nature of the problem, not by facts about the viability of a particular solution. Analysis based solely on facts will not identify inconsistencies and will only make real integration nearly impossible. Even if issues of fact do arise, it's extremely difficult to obtain an objective assessment of fact-based issues. Under these conditions, it is not surprising that for most corporations the process of developing strategy is neither very efficient nor very effectual.

What are the options? Getting rid of all data analysis staff groups is not the answer. Neither is assigning only one person the responsibility of formulating a strategy for each area. The appropriate solution is a careful redesign of the process of formulating strategy.

Patchwork changes made on an incremental basis won't work. All the factors that inhibit innovation—such as those created by abuses of information, staff, and organization—must be considered. The process must be established as an integrated system, and the organizational roles must be clearly spelled out. We'll examine the characteristics of one such system in the next chapter.

REFERENCES

1. Rosenthal, R., "On the Social Psychology of the Psychological Experiment: The Experimenter's Hypothesis as an Unintended Determinant of Experimental Results," *American Scientist*, June 1963, p. 268.

2. Caldwell, G. T., "Corporate Planning in Canada: An Overview," The Conference Board of Canada, 1975.

3. Lucado, W. E., "Corporate Planning—A Current Status Report," *Managerial Planning*, November–December 1974, p. 27.

4. Steiner, G. A., and H. Schollhammer, "Pitfalls in Multi-National Long Range Planning," *Long Range Planning*, April 1975, p. 2.

4

Removing Roadblocks to Innovation: One Company's Story

A powerful idea communicates some of its strength to him who challenges it. —MARCEL PROUST

In the mid-1970s, Basic Materials, Inc., the pseudonym for a major diversified industrial materials producer with sales of some $2 billion in 1975, faced a major strategic hurdle. Early in the decade, the company had established a number of venture teams, each staffed with functionally varied managers, to create profitable businesses from promising ideas that the company's R&D laboratories uncovered. One of these teams had been charged with guiding a revolutionary new material, dubbed "Super-Stuff," through development, production, test marketing, and finally distribution. Two key strategic issues confronted the Super-Stuff venture team. (1) Should Basic Materials be in the business of producing and selling Super-Stuff only as an unconverted material, or should it manufacture, fabricate, and sell finished Super-Stuff products? (2) If finished products were manufactured, should the company target its resources to develop a product for a single, large, and potentially profitable market, or should it pursue multiple markets simultaneously?

A classic set of strategic problems had to be overcome for

Super-Stuff to emerge as the cornerstone of a new business for Basic Materials. The saga begins deep in the company's R&D laboratories: The birth of a unique product concept with vast potential usually requires years of effort by key personnel and substantial investment of corporate resources. Those proponents most deeply involved in the viability of the concept face a series of uphill struggles to keep project funding alive, to overcome the constraints of regulatory compliance, and to deal with the uncertain economic climate. Finally, having surmounted these obstacles, the parent company is confronted with a major decision: how best to capitalize on the business potential of its innovation. This decision itself must constitute the most farsighted, innovative thinking of planners, for once a product is released on the open market, can imitations or even *better* innovations be far behind?

Basic Materials is a company with a tradition of innovative excellence. For many years the company has invested more of its sales revenues in R&D programs than its competitors and is today recognized as a pioneer in several areas of new technology. The company's experience in launching these new programs had made management well aware of the many pitfalls that can suddenly spring up. If Super-Stuff was to achieve its business potential, the management group charged with its development would have to blend strong capabilities not only in R&D but also in production, marketing, and finance. The company's venture-team concept was designed to do just that.

Managers who have witnessed or participated in efforts to develop a business based on a totally new product concept are all too familiar with how heated things can become in establishing priorities that integrate diverse perspectives. How well they know that these conflicts can lead to indecisive wheelspinning, strategically senseless political compromises, or dictatorial decisions. Hence the corporate mandate to the Super-Stuff team—to come up with a strategy that would be acceptable to the corporate executive committee, to avoid turning the venture group into fragmented, conflicting coalitions, and to be successful—carried with it considerable risk of failure.

The Super-Stuff team accomplished its task, and it did so in a highly professional fashion. Basic Materials attributes much of the team's success to a radically different planning methodology called Strategic Assumptions Analysis. Let's examine why there is a need for such a planning tool and how the company's success emanated from its use.

Underpinnings of Strategic Assumptions Analysis

As we have seen in previous chapters and in the brief analysis of the Basic Materials problem, most companies today face a number of complex organizational and external problems that inhibit innovative performance. Government regulation shows few signs of loosening its stranglehold on virtually all industrial sectors and, ultimately, on the pocketbooks of all consumers. Imaginative, though sporadic and often short-lived, employee-motivation programs have failed to stem the tide of rising absenteeism and waning worker morale. The widening consumer movement and the increasing aggressiveness of foreign business ventures are taking their toll on the profits of American business. And soaring inflation is contributing to the steady erosion of U.S. productivity. Combine these external pressures with internal organizational conflicts and we find ourselves confronted with a seemingly impenetrable obstacle to developing new product ideas and innovative ways to exploit them. Once again, however, I'll posit the belief that the executives of U.S. businesses should ask themselves whether they are doing all they can to avoid these pitfalls.

Strategic Assumptions Analysis (SAA) is a new process that was specifically designed to overcome many of the internal organizational obstacles to innovation that we've examined previously: ineffective staff involvement, inappropriate organizational structure, and incorrect use of information. We shall examine ways to deal systematically with specific external obstacles in Chapter 6.

In building any organizational strategy, there is an express need to ensure that three elements of the decision-making process are explicitly integrated: (1) the *strategy* itself, (2) the *data* that support the strategy, and (3) the underlying *assumptions* from which the strategy can be logically deduced.

My experience with corporate planning activities suggests that by far the greatest amount of time is spent designing strategies, with a little effort devoted to data collection to justify the strategy, and almost no time spent defining the assumptions upon which the strategy deductively rests. Because assumptions analysis is largely ignored, there is often no objective means to assess the tradeoffs among alternative strategies. And because data can be selectively collected and interpreted to establish the credibility of almost any reasonable strategy, the decision process often deteriorates to a state in which the various corporate groups that make up planning committees hoard tomes of data they require to make the case for the strategy they would like to have implemented. Deductive decision-making processes are nonexistent in this situation, which makes it almost impossible to evaluate the richness of each proposed strategy or to synthesize different strategies into a new one based on an integration of common assumptions. Instead, the decision is resolved by political compromises, using portions of each strategy to produce one that is often less effective than any of those proposed. Synergy, in this muddled state of confusion, is unthinkable.

One of the problems Basic Materials faced in its planning effort was that its executives were unaware of the impacts the implicitly or explicitly stated assumptions about its strategic options had on the effectiveness of those options. When the

Super-Stuff venture team was first assembled, its members had discussed many possible business strategies and had provided justifications for each option. Since a good case could be made for each of the options, the team had trouble reaching agreement on what to do. Further analysis of the options didn't seem to make the correct choice any more apparent. The group found itself at a strategic impasse. Sound familiar?

Two key premises, which are designed to deal with this dilemma, underlie Strategic Assumptions Analysis.

1. A successful strategy formulation process must give highest priority to *integrating the diverse perspectives* of managers, rather than *evaluating specific options* that are proposed.

2. This strategy integration can be achieved by concentrating on identifying acceptable and unacceptable *assumptions* that underlie the various strategy options.

The central feature of Strategic Assumptions Analysis is the use of explicitly identified assumptions as a basis for defining strategy. The process uses data analysis as a vehicle to link strategy with assumptions, instead of as a final evaluation of a particular strategy's validity. Once assumptions are agreed upon, the final strategy can be developed in a logical, deductive manner. However, if the assumptions buttressing the various strategies are neither understood nor accepted by the managers involved, no amount of data analysis will convince anyone as to why one strategy option should be pursued over another.

Most strategy formulation processes deal with assumptions, but in a way that seems to me to be ineffective. Typically, a list of specific assumptions about environmental and organizational conditions is generated very early in the game. These assumptions act as planning parameters, in that they provide the ground rules and constraints upon which a strategy is to be built. Such an assumptions list will normally include items like inflation rates, energy costs, and GNP growth rates. Thus assumptions are specified in the beginning of the process to narrow the range of options that would be considered in subsequent phases of analysis.

So what's so different about Strategic Assumptions Analysis? For one thing, SAA reverses the order and logic of the entire approach—actually stands much of the conventional wisdom about strategy formulation on its head! The SAA approach begins by identifying strategy options, rather than by identifying broad assumptions. There are some compelling reasons for getting strategy alternatives out on the table early in the process:

- *Good managers constantly think about solutions.* Therefore, in order to maximize productivity, managers should be encouraged to share ideas in as comfortable a setting as possible.
- *Different experiences and job perspectives lead logically to different solution possibilities.* These perspectives should surface explicitly at the beginning of the process, when they can have the strongest impact on the events to follow.
- *Managers have biases about strategy options.* By bringing these biases to the group's attention, the process can directly address points of agreement and disagreement.

Once the initial strategy options have been identified, SAA addresses critical issues associated with the assumptions, but from a fundamentally different perspective than most managers are accustomed to in dealing with them. Rather than defining broad assumptions that act as parameters within which every strategy solution must fit, a specific set of assumptions is developed for each strategy option.

These lists of assumptions have special significance in the SAA process, because many of them may be invalid. Each list is a statement about conditions that ought to exist if the associated strategy is to be successful. Instead of defining a group of valid assumptions and deducing strategies, the process accepts the validity of the strategy and deduces the assumptions. Why should we reverse the causal relationship between assumptions and strategies at this stage of the process? Three reasons stand out:

- *Broad-based assumptions do little to shape most strategies.* Because they are derived from such a high level of generality, broadly defined assumptions seldom shed light on how to resolve specific differences among the strategy options being considered.
- *The implied and often unspoken assumptions that underlie a strategy are forced to the surface.* Since the search is for completeness of an assumption base, conditions that clearly support a strategy option can be counterbalanced by those that clearly refute it.
- *New strategy options can be identified.* Assumptions that are neither clearly valid nor clearly invalid can be utilized in the negated form to generate new strategy options for consideration.

For example, in the early 1970s, when General Motors was developing its R&D strategy to meet federal pollution standards for its next generation of automobiles, GM executives undoubtedly made assumptions about the link between technology options and success in meeting the standards. This is an accepted practice, but the analysis probably stopped there. Had all the assumptions that were implied by each strategic option been examined using an SAA approach, perhaps GM would not have become committed to the catalytic converter as its answer to the problem. Compared with the stratified-charge approach to meeting pollution standards (the strategy Chrysler wanted to follow at the time), the catalytic converter was substantially less fuel-efficient (an implied assumption about further gasoline availability and cost) and required unleaded gasoline (an implied assumption about solutions that would not be applicable outside the U.S. car market). Strategic Assumptions Analysis helps uncover the "latent land mines" that may accompany solutions.

Likewise, had Edwin H. Land evaluated his earlier assumption that instant movies are a logical extension of instant photographs and that their time is now, Polaroid would probably not currently be struggling to unload its enormous inventory of Polavision instant movie systems. Although the concept of instant movies may have rested on valid assumptions about technology and production, it apparently rests on some false assumptions about consumer needs.

When the process of generating strategy options and their supporting assumptions has been completed, managers create a pool of the entire list of assumptions from every strategy and begin a process of weeding out those they are not willing to use as a basis for generating a final strategy. At this point each assumption's validity becomes critical. The issue—what is the group willing to accept as the set of assumptions that drives the final solution?—must be addressed. When these choices have been made, the group develops a final strategy by matching options with the assumptions that are chosen. This final stage possesses several important benefits not obtainable in more traditional processes.

- *Assumptions specification is directly relevant to the strategy.* Because all the assumptions being considered were supportive of at least one primary strategy option, they provide critical information on the appropriate structure of the final strategy.
- *The final strategy is not a compromise of elements in the initial options.* Because the strategy is developed directly from the final pool of assumptions, it is designed as an integrated whole.

- *Cost of error can be assessed.* Since the final strategy is logically tied to a set of assumptions, the costs can be estimated for the inappropriate implementation of a strategy, if the assumptions on which it was based fail to materialize.
- *Conditions that dictate strategy updates can be defined.* An assumptions-tracking system can be established to collect and report essential information relevant to the validity of key assumptions. Such a monitoring system can trigger the reconsideration and possible revision of the enacted strategy.

Let's now look at how the venture team was able to systematically design a viable strategy for Super-Stuff with the help of Strategic Assumptions Analysis.

Basic Materials, Inc.

One of the more imposing strengths of Basic Materials is its control of significant quantities of a major resource that is used extensively in most of its products. Because the company commands cost advantages in this basic resource, nearly all its businesses derive, in one way or another, from the resource. Figure 2 illustrates how these businesses are defined by products that represent various stages of conversion of the key resource.

The levels of profitability of the various businesses vary directly with the cost base attributable to the key resource component. Thus, of the three basic strategy options identified for downstream vertical integration, Basic Materials has consistently been most successful in businesses in which the conversion of product form is lowest, that is, sale of the product in raw form.

The commodity orientation of the corporation's products,

Figure 2. Business clusters: Basic Materials, Inc.

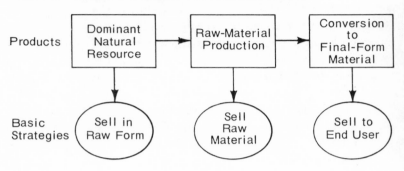

combined with an inherent price cyclicality in the industrial sector in which the company has participated, has led to wide swings in annual company profits. This situation bothered the company's senior managers. In response, they decided to try to develop new businesses in areas that would reduce the profit swings for the entire organization. Venture teams such as the Super-Stuff group were established to develop ideas that Basic Materials had uncovered but had previously not chosen to pursue.

The Super-Stuff Venture Group

One of the first venture possibilities the teams identified involved Super-Stuff, a revolutionary material technology that had been developed by the Basic Materials R&D laboratory. As shown in Figure 3, the material was actually a hybrid raw material composed of both the core natural material and other natural resources. Except that Super-Stuff could not be sold as a raw natural resource material, the business development issues surrounding the product were virtually identical to those the company faced with its traditional downstream operations. This situation had the significant effect of allowing senior management the comfort of understanding the nature of development options, and the risks associated with each.

Super-Stuff possessed some exceptional characteristics. It was clearly less dependent on the key natural resource than were most of the company's other products. Moreover, management know-how appeared to be directly translatable to the new venture. The most important consideration, however, was that the material appeared to have unique characteristics possessed by no other existing material.

As a beverage container material, Super-Stuff offered great possibilities. Besides offering economic advantages over existing containers, Super-Stuff insulated beverages better than metal cans, and so the beverages would stay colder longer. Hence management saw the burgeoning beverage industry as a prime candidate for initial exploitation of Super-Stuff. Its properties also suggested that it could revolutionize the convenience-food industry by providing an attractive frozen-dinner tray that could be heated in either conventional or microwave ovens. This would be a major advance over aluminum trays, which are ineffective in increasingly popular microwave ovens. In addition, Super-Stuff's strength-to-weight ratio attracted the immediate, enthusiastic attention of U.S. and foreign auto makers. This group envisioned the product as a substitute for many plastic and even metal auto

Figure 3. Options for the Super-Stuff venture group.

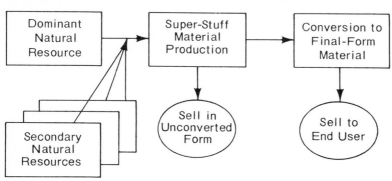

parts, thus helping achieve lighter and more fuel-efficient auto designs. Some farsighted Basic Materials executives even courted the early inquiries of government agencies interested in Super-Stuff as a highly adaptable building material, suitable for low-income housing in third-world nations. "Think of the possibilities," ventured one executive. "Complete walls and ceilings—strong, lightweight, and inexpensive—from which door and window openings can literally be cut at will with a saw." The potential of this revolutionary product was staggering.

Moreover, Super-Stuff's properties suggested the possibility of profit margins substantially more attractive than those of the commodity markets in which Basic Materials had traditionally competed. Management also recognized the possibility of considerably less cyclicality in some of Super-Stuff's potential end-use market applications. The Super-Stuff management team was thus established as the flagship of the venture concept. The corporation provided the group with staff and financial resources well above those allocated for any other venture project. Super-Stuff had obviously caught senior management's eye. But still ahead lay the pivotal task of deciding how to move the product from prototype development through large-scale production to finished-product manufacturing and distribution.

Since senior management was anxious to reduce the company's dependence on cyclical commodity businesses, the venture group decided that control of conversion would maximize that possibility; hence no Super-Stuff material would be sold unconverted. After an investigation of end-use market possibilities for Super-Stuff, the group identified beverage containers as an especially large, ripe market. Therefore, the group decided to concentrate its efforts on licking the technology problems in order to produce a functional product for this large market—in effect, taking a long-range rifle shot at one high-potential sector.

Four years after the Super-Stuff venture group initiated its strategy, however, the management's outlook was not nearly as optimistic as it had been at the start. Significant financial resources had been invested in the project, and expenses were tripling every year. The increasing rate of expenditures was not excessive; in fact, spending levels were only slightly above the original plan. But the program for delivering functional products that could be tested in the market was far behind schedule. Technological problems continued to surface, and somehow the light at the end of the tunnel never seemed to grow any brighter. In the last two years the estimated time to market entry hadn't changed. As quickly as one problem was solved, a new, unanticipated one would emerge.

To compound these problems, the target container market looked less and less attractive as time wore on. The problem had nothing to do with the estimated economics of the Super-Stuff beverage container; no one had reliable estimates of what the full-scale production costs might be. The rising storm cloud was the strong possibility of government regulation of beverage containers, a development that raised the distinct possibility that Super-Stuff's maiden market voyage might be canceled entirely.

The combination of these factors was extremely disconcerting to the company's senior management. The group was disturbed about the viability of the rifle-shot strategy in the rather unstable container market. The Super-Stuff venture team was worried as well about whether it was headed in the right direction. Therefore, the team agreed to rethink the entire strategy from scratch. They decided to use Strategic Assumptions Analysis to reexamine and possibly redefine the Super-Stuff venture. This reassessment required four months and involved approximately 30 percent of the efforts of a ten-member management group, comprising those with project leadership for the venture. Here's how it worked.

Strategic Assumptions Analysis and the Super-Stuff Strategy Problem

Figure 4 is a diagram of the Strategic Assumptions Analysis process. The analysis comprises three major phases: (1) identification of "pure" strategy options (first stage), (2) generation of assumptions and additional strategy options (middle three stages), and (3) integration into final solution (final three stages).

Stage 1. Define Basic Strategy Options

The basis on which the strategy options are created depends on the perspectives of the management groups involved in the decision and the issues relevant to the problem. In some cases an organizational perspective might be critical—for example, R&D versus Marketing versus Financial Planning. In others, strategy might be inspired by business philosophy—for exam-

Figure 4.   The Strategic Assumptions Analysis process.

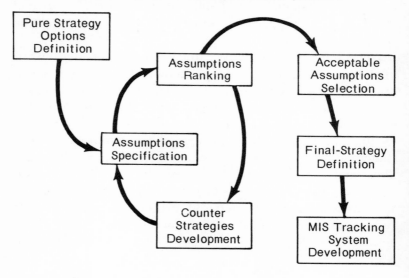

ple, aggressive new business development versus support of basic operations. Team members are selected carefully to provide as broad a perspective and as divergent a set of views as possible on alternative options for the strategy directions.

With the assistance of an outside consulting group to administer SAA, the Super-Stuff team met to identify the fundamental tacks it felt the Super-Stuff business could take. During these discussions, four functional management groups were represented on the Super-Stuff team:

1. *R&D.* The members of this group were the most threatened by the turn of events leading to the strategy reassessment. They believed that progress was being made on technological developments of Super-Stuff and that their efforts would be rewarded if their colleagues remained patient.

2. *Marketing.* The members of this group were upset over the promises they had made to potential customers in the container market. They believed that continued failure to live up to those promises was undermining the department's credibility, and they blamed R&D for the tension. They felt that their department was being forced to tread water too long because of the technological problems. They sought a strategy revision that would permit them to aggressively develop market opportunities somewhere—anywhere.

3. *Manufacturing.* The members of this group were tired of practicing Super-Stuff manufacturing techniques using bench-scale facilities. They were eager to accelerate toward full-scale operating capabilities in order to obtain manufacturing experience on producing the material and converting it into functional products.

4. *Financial Analysis.* This group was nervous over the validity of the data being used to justify capital expenditure appropriation requests. The data could easily be attacked by senior management when the next request for a major capital expansion in the project was made. Naturally the group didn't want its professional credibility undermined by such attacks.

An opening meeting flushed out this diversity of views fairly well. Since the first stage of SAA encourages such diversity, the tensions that might normally surround conflicting views were substantially less than the team had expected. Group discussions led to the identification of four strategy options that would be used to initiate the Strategic Assumptions Analysis process. These were:

1. *Continue on the present course.* This option involved complete control of the material manufacturing process as well as the converting operation. Under the control orientation, efforts would be focused on a single target market that had the attractive size and profitability characteristics the company desired. Kodak's strategy in the photography market illustrated a successful prototype.

2. *License the converting.* In this strategy the company would develop the converting technology for use of the material in several markets. However, the manufacturing of finished products through the conversion process would be licensed to a number of companies interested in such a business. Du Pont's fiber business was considered a prototype for this strategy.

3. *Let the market develop converting applications.* Under this strategy the company would concentrate on material manufacturing only. It would focus its R&D effort on producing Super-Stuff alloys that had a variety of special properties and economic characteristics. The way Super-Stuff would be used to supply end markets, however, would not be an area in which the company would invest its resources. Owens-Corning's marketing of Fiberglas was a prototype for this strategy.

4. *Sell the business.* This strategy was based on the perspective that other companies would be in a better position to successfully overcome the downstream marketing problems that had to be solved in order to achieve Super-Stuff's profit potential. Rather than allowing the potential business oppor-

tunity to lag because it didn't fit company management expertise, this strategy was based on selling the venture. General
Electric's strategy for selling small businesses that don't fit its
corporate parameters was a prototype for this strategy.

Naturally, each of the four basic strategies had allies within
the ten-member team. Thus the group was divided according
to each member's belief that a particular philosophy was the
right direction in which to proceed. For the next several
phases of Strategic Assumptions Analysis, these advocacy
teams operated independently, each group being charged
with the responsibility of drawing out the implications of the
particular strategy direction.

Stage 2. Identify the Assumptions

In the second stage of SAA, Super-Stuff team members articulated all the assumptions that logically underlay each
strategy option. Each team assumed that its strategy was correct and searched for all the logically consistent assumptions
that would justify their plan. Consequently, some of the assumptions were likely to be invalid. It is precisely this mix of
valid and invalid assumptions for each strategy that explains
their differences and is the reason that they cannot all be optimal simultaneously. To be sure no team stacked the deck for
its strategy by conveniently "forgetting" to include a few
damaging assumptions, each team reviewed the assumptions
lists of the others and added to them where necessary.

In order to articulate every possible assumption, it was
necessary to systematically identify all the groups inside and
outside the organization whose behavior would affect the success of the particular strategy option. These groups are called
stakeholders. A stakeholder is any group that has a significant
stake in the ultimate outcome of a particular strategy. Typically these groups include customers, consumerists, competitors, government agencies, suppliers, senior management,
other divisions within the company, and the like. By formulat-

ing a comprehensive list of these groups, managers can create comparative assumptions about each strategy option, thus substantially reducing the probability that key stakeholders will be excluded from consideration. Assumptions that support a particular strategy but that cannot be attributed to the behavior of a particular stakeholder—for example, energy costs, unemployment, and inflation rates—are defined as "environmental assumptions."

Figure 5 represents the relationship of Super-Stuff's core stakeholders to the venture issue. The advocates of each strategy option must make assumptions about the behavior of each stakeholder group with respect to its Super-Stuff

Figure 5. Super-Stuff's core stakeholders.

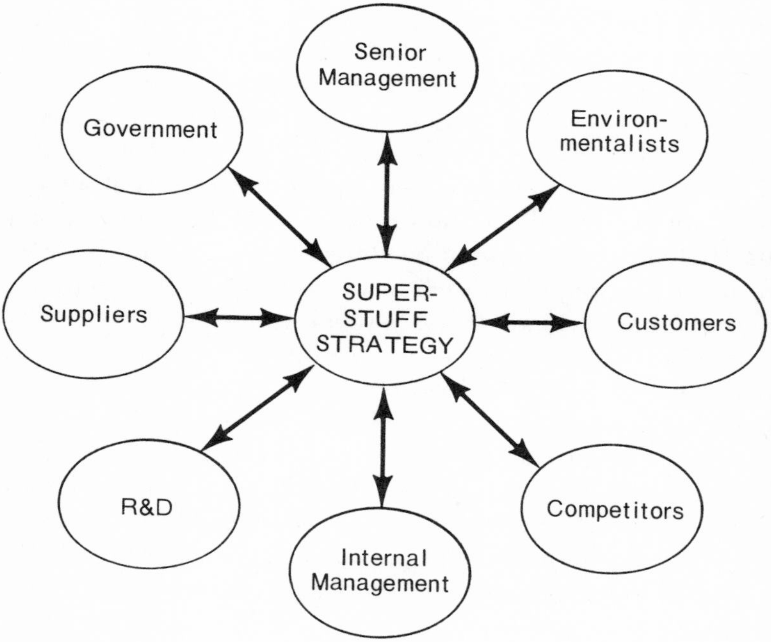

strategy. These assumptions are statements about the behavior of each stakeholder group that would most guarantee the success of the particular strategy. In addition, each team is permitted to identify special stakeholders whose behavior was particularly important to its strategy. For example, for the "sell the business" strategy, assumptions about the purchaser of the business were obviously important.

Before finalizing the lists of stakeholder and environmental assumptions, a test of the relevancy of each assumption was conducted. This is done simply by stating the assumption in its negated form. When the assumption is negated, the proposed strategy ought to be altered. In other words, if a negated assumption reduces the predicted performance of a strategy option but doesn't change the structure of the strategy, then the original assumption enhances the strategy's performance but doesn't fundamentally drive the proposed strategy. By eliminating such noncritical assumptions, a significantly reduced list of core assumptions remains as the fundamental underpinning of each strategy.

To illustrate the assumptions-negation test, several of the strategy advocacy teams made assumptions about the lack of government regulations in particular areas. For the team developing the rifle-shot strategy in the beverage container market, the assumption that federal regulations would not restrict one-way containers was critical. If the assumption were negated (in other words, if regulations were imposed), the strategy would be destroyed. However, for the strategy in which the market developed end-use applications for Super-Stuff material, regulations affecting particular markets could be imposed without weakening the basic strategy; hence these assumptions could be eliminated from further consideration.

Finally, to ensure completeness of stakeholder assumptions, each Super-Stuff strategy team organized the assumptions into a hierarchy of statement generality, as illustrated in Figure 6.

Figure 6. Hierarchical structure of assumptions specifications.

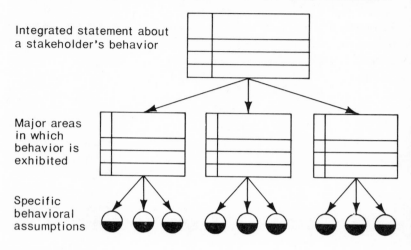

Integrated statement about
a stakeholder's behavior

Major areas
in which
behavior is
exhibited

Specific
behavioral
assumptions

At the highest level, one integrated statement is formulated for each stakeholder in order to capture the basic behavioral assumption a strategy implies. This collective statement should then be divisible into major areas in which such behavior is exhibited and finally into specific assumptions about the stakeholder's actions.

For example, the federal government may be assumed to act in an increasingly strict regulatory role with regard to environmental quality. This posture manifests itself in regulating the exploitation of the nation's natural resources, the volume of highway litter, and the quantity of industrial waste elimination. Specifically, this posture becomes critical to Super-Stuff's future for the beverage container strategy. For example, nonreturnable beverage containers may be outlawed, all future beverage containers might have to be biodegradable, and even the company's use of its key natural resource may be subject to tighter government control.

By creating such a hierarchy, areas of incomplete assumptions definition can be identified and enhanced. Moreover, the

three levels can be made more compatible through this arrangement. For example, government behavior with respect to
Super-Stuff's use in the beverage industry could be analyzed
according to assumptions regarding legislative, regulatory,
and fiscal aspects. This structure also permits the review and
comparative assessment of assumptions at different levels of
detail. Comparing the essential differences among strategies
need not go into excessive detail if the primary message can
be summarized in a more aggregate form.

Stage 3. Assess Each Strategy's Assumptions

Next, the Super-Stuff team assessed each assumption for
importance and *validity*. The Beliefs Assessment process,
which is explained in Chapter 5, is used for this purpose. The
outcome of this activity is represented by a two-dimensional
scale, as shown in Figure 7. This graph indicates the simul-
taneous assessments of the degree of confidence that a particular assumption is true as stated (that is, its validity is measured) and the degree to which the strategy would be
weakened if the assumption were found to be invalid (that is,
its importance is measured).

Figure 7. Importance-validity map.

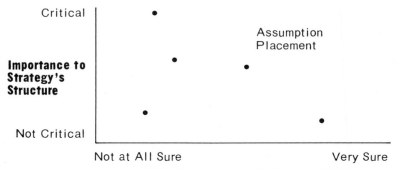

These assessments are made both at an aggregate stakeholder level and at more detailed levels for each stakeholder. This enables stakeholder assumptions graphs to be generated for each strategy at different levels of detail. Such graphs are shown in Figure 8. The process is conducted in order to maximize the integration of the experience and expertise of managers who deal with the assumptions, and, simultaneously, to incorporate a basis for further data analysis and testing of the managerial perceptions.

Two things are readily apparent from the maps in Figure 8. First, different stakeholders are important for each strategy. Second, the degree of certainty about assumptions for each stakeholder's behavior is very different for the two strategies. The then-current venture strategy (complete control) shows that the assumptions were highly uncertain about the most important stakeholders; that is, government behavior and R&D breakthroughs. Thus the strategy was effectively one of high risk and low control. The alternative strategy identified a different group of stakeholders as most important, and their behaviors were somewhat more certain. As a result, the alternative was one of lower risk and greater control. This is not to say

Figure 8. Stakeholder assumptions for two strategies.

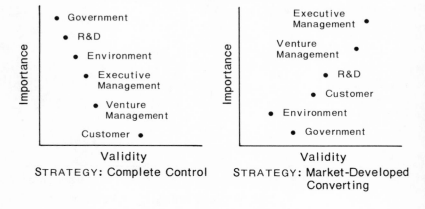

STRATEGY: Complete Control   STRATEGY: Market-Developed
                                            Converting

that one of the strategies was necessarily better than the other; but it does say that in order to justify the increased risk, the potential return for adopting the current strategy should have been substantially higher than for the particular alternative. Analysis of the detailed specific behavioral assumptions helped clarify the cause of this outcome.

Stage 4. Search for Counterstrategies

The search for counterstrategies is essentially a brainstorming session in which team members must decide whether they are able to use the assumptions information they've developed from the assumptions graphs in Stage 3 to define additional, exhaustive strategy options. They can now pool assumptions from all four strategy options and classify the assumptions according to, for example, those that caused the greatest degree of uncertainty of their validity, or those that were most important to the success of a particular option.

The key assumptions to be addressed here are those whose validity is found to be highly uncertain. These assumptions could be either valid or invalid—at this point no one knows for sure. Since managers are generally trained to avoid uncertainty, these assumptions probably were not carefully examined before the process began. Here they will be. Since this group of assumptions is highly uncertain, an equally plausible case could be made for their negation. For example, if some viable strategy rests on a Democratic victory in a presidential election, but that outcome is considered highly uncertain, one can make an equally plausible case for a Republican victory. In a more general sense, if all the highly uncertain assumptions created by any of the original strategy options are negated, then an opposite view of the world is created, one that is equally valid. The issue in the counterstrategy process centers on whether a new strategy can be created using some of these negated assumptions as a foundation. If so, the so-called "counterstrategy" is likely to be quite different from any proposed so far. Even if the full analysis of assumptions required to support the counterstrategy shows significant weaknesses (that is, many of the critical assumptions are invalid), some rich, new assumptions will almost certainly enter the pool for consideration in the final stages of strategy design.

As for Super-Stuff, the venture team found that assumptions about the role of R&D in the project were the least certain. A particularly vexing issue was whether R&D could be responsive to market needs in producing innovative converted products using the new material. R&D was considered to be weak in this area, but these assumptions were untested and thus highly uncertain. Therefore, a new set of assumptions was created around the theme that one of R&D's strongest capabilities concerned its ability to develop new innovation in converted-product form over a wide variety of products and markets. Using this set of assumptions as a basis, a new counterstrategy was developed. In it, two profit centers were created—a materials company and a converting company. The converting company was R&D-dominated and made profits largely because of its technological creativity in formulating and delivering technological innovation.

When the team had completely defined this counterstrategy, the members repeated the assumptions assessment process of Stage 3 for it. This process generated an entirely new set of assumptions, many of which were in completely different areas from those addressed in the original four pure strategies. Since the validity of a number of these counterassumptions was highly certain, they represented a considerable expansion of the pool of acceptable assumptions.

Stage 5. Agree on Acceptable "Core" Assumptions

At this point in the process, the Super-Stuff group has identified both pure strategy options and, through an assessment of the uncertain assumptions, has developed additional, or "counter," strategies for Super-Stuff. Stage 5 comprises a weeding, or purging, process. The team's objective is to identify those assumptions that it is prepared to use to design an integrated final strategy. Here again, the assumptions graphs defined in Stage 3 become central. Figure 9 identifies three important ones for consideration. Assumptions whose validity is highly certain—those in zone I—can be included in the final pool without discussion, regardless of their relative importance to driving strategies. Similarly, all clearly invalid assumptions—those in zone II—can be rejected.

The most interesting issues center on the group of highly uncertain assumptions. Each of the original strategy teams naturally wants its own set of "important but uncertain" assumptions included in the final pool. The more of such assumptions that are included in the final list, the more likely that the final strategy will reflect the basic thrust of the original position.

Figure 9. Assumptions selection.

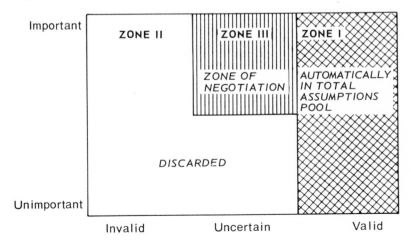

The unimportant assumptions can be dropped, because they have little impact on the key issues that shaped the definitions of the original strategy options. This leaves a group of important assumptions whose validity is highly uncertain. How can their treatment in the strategy design process be resolved? The first step is an attempt to modify the wording of these assumptions. Management must determine whether it is possible to change the statement in such a way that (1) the validity is much more certain, and (2) the rewording still fundamentally supports the original strategy that produced it. If both of these requirements can be met, the reformulated assumption enters the final pool. For example, a highly uncertain assumption such as "A beverage manufacturer will accept a single supplier of Super-Stuff cans" might be changed to read "A beverage manufacturer will accept a single supplier of Super-Stuff cans for up to 25 percent of its needs" and become a valid assumption.

On the other hand, if rewording fails to lessen the assumption's ambiguity, the team must decide if it is possible to perform short-term research or data analysis to clarify the ambiguity. If so, the analysis should be undertaken and the assumption included or excluded based on the results. For example, quick research can determine whether frozen-food companies are interested in replacing aluminum TV dinner trays with microwavable packaging.

If neither of these approaches is successful, then the assumption should be included in the pool on a conditional basis. Thereafter, any new strategy that requires the support of conditional assumptions must be designed in such a way that, until the validity of the assumptions has been established with greater confidence, dependence on those conditional assumptions is not critical. This is a form of contingency planning.

The Super-Stuff team integrated the assumptions into an effective pool for further strategy definition, as we'll see in

Stage 6. At the beginning of the assumptions integration process, team members still assumed the roles of their respective pure strategy teams. As the final strategy assumptions pool was taking shape, team members began to express an integrated perspective; that is, the pool was viewed as an asset without regard to the original strategy that generated it. From this stage forward the assumptions analysis was one undivided effort by the entire team.

Stage 6. Define the New Strategy

The vehicle the venture team used to design a new strategy for Super-Stuff, based on the final pool of core assumptions, is issue analysis. This process begins by identifying the critical issues that would have a major impact on the final strategy. Here an issue is a question stated in such a way that it can be answered *yes* or *no*. Once an issue is formulated, it is evaluated on an assumption-by-assumption basis for the entire pool of acceptable assumptions. Each assumption is examined to determine whether it supports the affirmative response to the issue, supports the negative response to the issue, or is unrelated to the issue's resolution. Thus the weight of the conclusions in the issue analysis enables answers to be provided for each issue. Analyzing the assumptions-driven answers to all the issues thus provides the key inputs necessary to define the appropriate strategy.

Figure 10 shows how the issue analysis process was conducted for one particular stakeholder on the issue of whether materials processing should ever be considered as a legitimate joint venture. Figure 11 follows the same issue analysis to conclusion by summarizing the issue position for each of the major stakeholders.

In all, 13 separate issues were analyzed using this process. As the process was being conducted, it was impressive to see agreement on an assumptions-based resolution to key questions that would affect the shaping of strategy. The team was

Figure 10. Issue analysis using executive management assumptions.

ISSUE: Should Materials Processing Be Joint Ventured?

ASSUMPTIONS ABOUT EXECUTIVE MANAGEMENT	POSITION ON ISSUE
1. Executive management seeks to add value to existing raw materials; it believes that risks are higher the further the final product is transformed from raw materials.	Yes
2. Executive management is not comfortable with a business based on one large purchaser; thus risk sharing is required.	Yes
3. The commercialization-decision criteria will be lower if capital requirements are less.	Yes
4. Executive management desires multiple converters of end products.	N/A
5. Executive management is willing to invest its own resources in converting technology if market opportunity is high.	No
6. Executive management wants to spend more of its own time on existing businesses and delegate noncore business management.	Yes

Overall Position: *Weak Yes*

completely unified in its efforts to draw out and resolve these issues through systematic examination of the assumptions base, rather than through political infighting.

More than one strategy may be created from this process, since the conditional assumptions identified in the preceding stage could impact on one or more issue positions and thus on the formulation of a final strategy. To test this, the team must conduct a sensitivity analysis in which the conditional assumptions, singly and in groups, are removed from the assumptions pool. If assumptions conditions cause basic changes in issue positions and in turn on strategy formulation, then the different strategies and their associated assumptions must each be considered.

Figure 11. Issue assessment among stakeholders for "joint venture of material processing."

	POSITION ON
STAKEHOLDER	ISSUE
Senior management	Weak yes
Converting customers	Strong yes
End-product customers	Strong yes
Government	Strong yes
R&D	Strong no

Overall Assessment: *Yes*

The method of evaluating strategy options is a cost-of-error analysis, as illustrated in Figure 12. The chart shows the cost estimates of errors that will occur if a particular strategy is adopted but a different set of assumptions actually turns out to be valid. Three kinds of errors are relevant for consideration: (1) real cost (RC)—the true and total impact of not adopting the best strategy; (2) visible cost (VC)—the amount of the real cost that management will be able to observe and tangibly evaluate; and (3) reversibility (R)—the degree to which errors in strategy could be rectified when the true situation was discovered.

Each of these calculations may be different and have a different importance to managers involved in the decision process. The ultimate choice of strategy is not likely to be easy, because the tradeoffs are complex. The basis of assessment, however, is likely to be far more sophisticated and useful than at similar stages of most strategy evaluation processes. For example, the Super-Stuff team was well aware that the real cost of selling the business could never be evaluated through visible costs, since the only data would be on what another company did with the concept. However, the visible cost and the real cost are both obvious if the rifle-shot approach is mistakenly tried in a market such as beverage containers—everyone can see the failure. With respect to reversibility, the rifle-shot approach can be reoriented fairly quickly (assuming

Figure 12. Cost evaluation of conditional assumptions.

Assumed Validity of Set of Assumptions		S_1	S_2	S_3
	A_1	CORRECT	ERROR RC = ? VC = ? R = ?	ERROR RC = ? VC = ? R = ?
	A_2	ERROR RC = ? VC = ? R = ?	CORRECT	ERROR RC = ? VC = ? R = ?
	A_3	ERROR RC = ? VC = ? R = ?	ERROR RC = ? VC = ? R = ?	CORRECT

Implementation Strategy

corporate capital is available), but the commitment to sell the business is irreversible.

Once the Super-Stuff team analyzed all the issues, members were able to design the final strategy. Company confidentiality prohibits a detailed discussion of the strategy's characteristics here; however, three aspects can be briefly discussed.

First, the new strategy led to a much stronger focus on managing the process of market development. Instead of monitoring only steps in R&D-related technological issues, the strategy for market penetration included continuous analysis of many market-oriented factors. Such factors as customer and competitor activities, primary consumer demand for related products, and actions of potential joint-venture partners were all part of this activity. The team designed a new and much more sophisticated management system in order to strengthen and facilitate this new focus.

Second, the new strategy dealt with the issue of product pricing. Because Basic Materials was a commodity-oriented company, it had little control over product pricing for its traditional businesses. The main problem the company faced was ensuring that price levels of its products provided an adequate margin for investment return. Because the new material provided unique opportunities for product positioning, the pricing strategy adopted by the Super-Stuff team was not directly oriented toward profit-margin considerations. Instead, market analyses were conducted to determine the economic value the product was expected to provide. Those markets with high economic value and low production and conversion costs became high-priority targets. Thus market attractiveness was related not only to the sales volume Super-Stuff could generate but to profit-margin possibilities as well.

Third, the final strategy concerned production of the material. The implicit strategy adopted up until the review was to build production facilities that would have the maximum economy of scale, and hence the lowest per unit cost of production. In conjunction with the revised thinking on pricing strategy, the venture team restudied all elements of production-facility size. It came to the conclusion that the biggest and most economic production facility was not necessarily the ideal size for the new strategy. It adopted a much more flexible production strategy, one that considered smaller units located strategically to serve both the general and the specialty needs that various markets might demand.

Stage 7. Implement the Strategy and Track Its Progress

The Super-Stuff team had completed the task of formulating a new strategy. It remained only to ask for the Corporate Executive Committee's approval of the plan and to set the strategy in action.

The proposed Super-Stuff business plan was a fairly dramatic departure from what was then in place. The venture team knew it faced a tough sell to the Executive Committee. The presentation of the plan to the Committee consisted of a systematic documentation of Strategic Assumptions Analysis and all the supporting assumptions on which the final strategy rested. Even the assumptions made about senior management were presented—causing considerable discussion.

The Executive Committee accepted the recommendations. And it went one step farther. The Committee identified one of the key assumptions in the plan and set a specific time by which the assumption had to be validated. The assumption involved customer commitments for Super-Stuff material in several different markets. Marching orders were clearly defined:

"Get the commitments by the specified date and you have a capital commitment for the business; otherwise the Super-Stuff venture will be terminated."

Nothing could have given a greater impetus to the start of the assumptions-tracking phase of the strategy than the corporate directive the team got. The response was immediate. R&D adjusted its focus to concentrate on the areas in which the stakes were highest. A new posture was established in market emphasis and customer negotiations. The new unified focus of the Super-Stuff team was impressive.

A key element of Strategic Assumptions Analysis is that it provides documentation for the agreements that are reached. As a result, along with the implementation of the new strategy, the Super-Stuff team was in a position to begin to monitor any changes in the critical assumptions on a continuous basis. Thus, as conditions changed, the strategy could be revised and updated on an as-needed basis. Emphasis was obviously greatest on assumptions about customer behavior, but other tracking systems were also established. This was recognized to be far more valuable than a periodic, radical revision, such as that which the team had previously undertaken.

Overall Assessment

In the real world, all endings are not happy. Such was the denouement of the story of Super-Stuff. Customer commitments could not be obtained by the date specified, and the program was phased out. However, this decision was made professionally and fairly. Everyone involved accepted it without ill feelings. The team believed it had been given a fair chance. Its only regret was that the SAA process wasn't instituted two years earlier; the results might have been different.

In the next chapter we'll examine some additional applications of Strategic Assumptions Analysis and address some associated critical issues that confront most executives in developing innovative business strategies.

5

Capitalizing on
Group Decision Making

I must create a system, or be enslaved by another man's;
I will not reason and compare; my business is to create.

—WILLIAM BLAKE

In Chapter 3, I noted that many companies are moving toward wider managerial participation in the process of formulating corporate strategies. I discussed the potential advantages this migration can provide, as well as the significant problems it can produce. Strategic Assumptions Analysis is designed to encourage the exchange of executive experiences and perspectives without having the strategy-building process deteriorate into win–lose battles when individual perspectives seem incompatible.

A key reason that Strategic Assumptions Analysis is able to encourage successful executive interaction is that it incorporates explicit step-by-step processes by which perceptions can be introduced, assessed, and resolved. On the basis of my experience with high-level corporate meetings, I've concluded that an effective balance rarely exists between organizing how things will be done and encouraging open, creative discussion. Too often the session is either a "rubber stamp" approval of work that has already been completed or a "bull session" that seems to inhibit conclusions. In either case the

106

payoff seldom justifies the substantial commitment of executive time required. Strategic Assumptions Analysis is designed to overcome these pitfalls.

The explicit roadmap that SAA provides for making complex decisions helps managers participate as a team, because they know the objectives that are to be achieved in each meeting. Instituting such a system signals top management's commitment to adopting new approaches, and that in itself can get the ball rolling. In addition to the structure that SAA provides, there are several companion techniques that augment the effectiveness of managerial participation even further.

Beliefs Assessment

Good managers possess good judgment; that is, they have the ability to formulate correct decisions even when all the facts are not at hand. Strategic Assumptions Analysis exploits this managerial ability by forcing judgmental decisions at critical points in the process, particularly when assumptions must be evaluated with respect to their *importance* to a strategy and their *validity*. Here, then, is where the diverse perspectives of managers must be integrated into overall strategic assessments.

Professor Thomas Saaty, a colleague at the Wharton Applied Research Center, has developed a new and powerful tool that helps induce the interaction among managers required to produce these important judgments. Saaty's approach has applications for a wide variety of decisions in addition to those addressed in Strategic Assumptions Analysis.[1] The process, which we call Beliefs Assessment, not only permits a constructive interchange of ideas among managers on the issues at hand, but also forces the discussions to be concluded in such a way that everyone knows what has been decided and why.

Let's illustrate how Beliefs Assessment works. For the sake

of consistency, we'll assess the beliefs of the Super-Stuff venture team at Basic Materials regarding one of the strategy options it developed early in its SAA. The option can be summarized as: Basic Materials controls both Super-Stuff material and end-product development and fabrication. Furthermore, the company would like to maintain a low introductory price and profit margin for Super-Stuff in order to quickly establish a high sales volume and ultimately achieve competitive advantages through economies of scale in production.

We enter the process when the Super-Stuff team has completed the second phase of SAA. That is, the team has identified stakeholders whose behavior will affect the success of this strategy, and its members have articulated the specific assumptions about the behavior of each stakeholder that would lead to the success of this particular strategy. Remember, these are the assumptions that make the best case for the strategy—they may or may not be valid.

In the third phase of the process, management must assess both the importance and the validity of each stakeholder assumption. Although there are likely to be more than four key stakeholders, for simplicity let us assume that the behaviors of only soft-drink bottlers, the brewing industry, can manufacturers, and federal regulatory agencies are relevant to this strategy. The team is now confronted with determining the relative importance of each group to the success of the "complete control" plan.

Judging Stakeholders' Importance

The Beliefs Assessment process begins by specifying an operationally meaningful criterion for the judgment of a single pair of items. For example, in judging the *importance* of the brewers' or the can manufacturers' behaviors to the strategy, one criterion could be, "If I had only five minutes to make a case for the full-control strategy based on a discussion of brewers' and manufacturers' behavioral assumptions, how much time would I allocate to each?"

After the judgment criterion has been defined, a Beliefs Assessment chart, as shown in Figure 13, is prepared. It is here that the consensus evaluations of the management group are recorded. Each cell in the chart will have a number in it when the process is completed, the number reflecting the group's judgment about the two specific items with respect to the criterion. For example, the "*" cell for the importance criterion would reflect "The proportion of time one would spend discussing bottlers' behavior versus manufacturers' behavior as a basis for defending the strategy's strength."

Several aspects of the assessment process are evident from the chart. First, judgments are made only on pairs of items, not on all stakeholders simultaneously. This feature is one of the greatest strengths of the process. Managers can concentrate their attention on a simple two-way comparison and develop the information for the overall assessment. In fact, Saaty has used certain mathematical properties of such pairwise relationships and a computer analysis routine to convert the individual judgments into an overall assessment weighting—

Figure 13.   Beliefs Assessment chart.

STAKEHOLDER \ STAKEHOLDER	Soft-Drink Bottlers	Brewing Industry	Can Manufacturers	Federal Agencies
Soft-Drink Bottlers			*	
Brewing Industry				
Can Manufacturers				
Federal Agencies				

percentage weights for the items that add to 100 percent—plus a quantitative estimate of the degree of internal consistency among the individual evaluations.

Second, not all pairs of the chart need to be evaluated by management. Obviously, the diagonal of cells from upper left to lower right needs no analysis, since each of these cells represents the relationship of an item being compared with itself. Furthermore, for each of the other comparisons, there is another cell with the same comparison in reverse. For example, the evaluation for the "*" cell in the soft-drink-bottlers row and the can-manufacturers column of Figure 13 is essentially the same as that for the cell at which the can-manufacturers row and the soft-drink-bottlers column intersect. Taking all this into account, the Beliefs Assessment process required six separate judgments for the four-stakeholder assessment.

The actual judgment process proceeds as follows. Suppose the Super-Stuff group was evaluating the relative importance of bottlers versus manufacturers for the low-price, high-volume, full-control strategy. Without prior discussion, each team member would specify a direction of dominance—for example, "The assumptions we made about the behaviors of manufacturers are more important to this strategy's success than those about the bottlers," or vice versa. If disagreements exist, members on each side of the issue would be allowed a limited and prespecified amount of time to explain their reasoning. Because the objectives of this activity are quite specific, the facts and interpretations of perceptions that cause the differences emerge quite quickly. When this task is completed, the entire group reaches consensus on the direction of dominance, and the principal reasons for the conclusion are recorded. Similar records are maintained for all major Beliefs Assessment judgments to allow later staff analysis and reinterpretation.

Let's say that Paul and Mark of the production and marketing departments, respectively, agreed that the importance of the bottlers dominated that of federal agencies. But Ron of R&D and Fran of finance believed that the importance of federal agencies was dominant. After the allotted time for discussion, the group members finally agreed that the importance of the bottlers to the success of the strategy slightly dominated the importance of federal agencies. They may have discovered that the reason for the difference of opinion is an unclear statement of specific elements of the strategy; for instance, a national marketing focus could make the difference in stakeholder importance.

Having determined the dominant stakeholder (the stakeholder judged in the pairwise comparison to be more important to the success of the full-control strategy), the team members each make an independent, pairwise *numerical* assessment as to the *magnitude* of the difference in importance between the two stakeholders. We use a nine-point scale to compare stakeholders. Rating numbers translate to judgments as follows:

1   means the two stakeholders are *equally* important.
3   means the stakeholder on the row is *weakly* more important than the stakeholder in the column.
5   means the stakeholder on the row is *moderately* more important than the stakeholder in the column.
7   means the stakeholder on the row is *strongly* more important than the stakeholder in the column.
9   means the stakeholder on the row is *absolutely* more important than the stakeholder in the column.

The scale is continuous; therefore any number between 1 and 9 can be used to designate compromise positions.

Once again, an organized discussion of the reasons for perceptual differences among members enables consensus. Reasons are recorded here as well. Occasionally, the group is not able to reach agreement, even after extensive discussion. When this happens, resolutions can be reached only by averaging judgments from the two diverse perspectives. But the process doesn't end with unsatisfactory compromise. Instead, staff groups undertake research projects to marshal the facts relevant to the areas of disagreement. The additional material would be presented in subsequent sessions to provide the management team with all the information when a final consensus is reached.

As each pair of stakeholder assumptions is completed, the information is recorded in two cells of the chart. In the intersecting cell in which the stakeholder on the row of the chart dominates the stakeholder in the column, the judgment is expressed as a whole number. For example, if the members of the Super-Stuff team are in consensus that the bottlers' behavior dominates the can manufacturers' behavior weakly (rating = 3), then in the intersection cell of the bottlers' row and the manufacturers' column, the team would record "3." Since manufacturers are three times bottlers, bottlers are ⅓ manufacturers. Thus, in the intersection cell of the manufacturers' row and the bottlers' column, the team would record "⅓," as illustrated in Figure 14. Had manufacturers been judged weakly more important than bottlers, the numbers would be reversed in the cells.

The aggregate pairwise judgments of the Super-Stuff team concerning the importance of all the stakeholders are similarly represented in Figure 15. We find from this chart the following dominance relationships:

Bottlers dominate manufacturers weakly (3)
Brewers dominate manufacturers moderately to strongly (6)
Brewers dominate bottlers weakly to moderately (4)
Bottlers dominate feds weakly to moderately (4)
Brewers dominate feds strongly (7)
Manufacturers dominate feds equally to weakly (2)

Figure 14. One judgment in the Beliefs Assessment chart.

STAKEHOLDER / STAKEHOLDER	Soft-Drink Bottlers	Brewing Industry	Can Manufacturers	Federal Agencies
Soft-Drink Bottlers	1		3	
Brewing Industry		1		
Can Manufacturers	$1/3$		1	
Federal Agencies				1

Figure 15. Completed Beliefs Assessment chart.

STAKEHOLDER / STAKEHOLDER	Soft-Drink Bottlers	Brewing Industry	Can Manufacturers	Federal Agencies
Soft-Drink Bottlers	1	$1/4$	3	4
Brewing Industry	4	1	6	7
Can Manufacturers	$1/3$	$1/6$	1	2
Federal Agencies	$1/4$	$1/7$	$1/2$	1

The computer analysis takes care of the aggregation of the judgments. In this particular example, the final percentage weights are:

Soft-drink bottlers	22%
Brewing industry	62
Can manufacturers	10
Federal agencies	6
	100

Thus, the brewing industry is judged by the Super-Stuff team to be the most important stakeholder to the success of the full-control Super-Stuff strategy.

Judging the Certainty of the Assumptions

The Super-Stuff team utilized the same pairwise judgmental technique to determine the *certainty* of each assumption's validity that it did to ascertain the importance of each stakeholder to the success of a particular strategy. For example, in considering the full-control strategy, the Super-Stuff team articulated, among others, the following assumptions that would logically imply the strategy:

1. If Basic Materials manufactures Super-Stuff, extensive profit opportunities exist for marketing finished products.
2. Corporate capital expenditures on plants and equipment require a viable product.
3. End-use customers will accept Basic Materials as the sole Super-Stuff supplier.
4. Technological obsolescence of Super-Stuff is assured within 15 years.

Once again, we employ the judgmental chart to record the consensus ratings of the certainty of each assumption's validity. However, team members must be sure to note the direction of certainty. That is, a judgmental rating of 9 could indicate strong certainty that an assumption is true, or it could mean strong certainty that an assumption is false. Low num-

Figure 16.   Beliefs Assessment chart for assumptions validity.

ASSUMPTION / ASSUMPTION	Abundant Opportunities	Capital/Viable Product	Sole Supplier	Obsolescence
Abundant Opportunities	1			
Capital/Viable Product		1		
Sole Supplier			1	
Obsolescence				1

bers indicate uncertainty, not that the assumption is untrue.

The assumptions-validity calculations (showing the degree to which each assumption's truth or falseness is judged more certain than that of a second assumption) are represented in Figure 16.

After determining the dominant direction of validity of each assumption (true or false) by the usual method, team members make pairwise judgments as to the certainty. For example, the group is weakly to moderately more certain that the sole-supplier assumption is true than that the obsolescence assumption is true by a rating of 4. After completing this comparison technique for all pairs, the chart would resemble Figure 17. The final percentage weights from this comparison are:

Abundant opportunities	61%
Capital/viable product	24
Sole supplier	10
Obsolescence	5
	100%

Figure 17. Completed Beliefs Assessment chart.

ASSUMPTION	Abundant Opportunities	Capital/Viable Product	Sole Supplier	Obsolescence
Abundant Opportunities	1	5	6	7
Capital/Viable Product	$1/5$	1	4	6
Sole Supplier	$1/6$	$1/4$	1	4
Obsolescence	$1/7$	$1/6$	$1/4$	1

From this evaluation, the team learns that it judges abundant opportunities to be the most certainly true of the four assumptions; whereas the certainty that Super-Stuff will become obsolete within 15 years is relatively low.

The team can now use the results of these analyses of stakeholder importance and assumptions validity to construct assumptions graphs, which is undertaken in Stage 5 of Strategic Assumptions Analysis. Eventually, this information is used to gather a pool of acceptable assumptions from which the team designs a new strategy. These phases of Strategic Assumptions Analysis were presented in Chapter 4.

Beliefs Assessment is designed to enrich management's understanding of why a particular strategy is most attractive and of the assumptions on which the strategies rely. The process provides a starting point for refining existing strategies or formulating new ones. The qualitative results derive from the insights managers gain through the process of negotiation. But the quantitative outcome is far less important than the discussion that produced it. Beliefs Assessment forces managers to identify and reveal their supporting arguments in order to reach agreement; therefore the arguments themselves become refined in the process. Consequently, the process itself results in an improved product in terms of the strategy.

From systematic conflict resolution, we move now to another factor that is critical to the effectiveness of managerial cooperation, the success of any strategy formulation technique, and ultimately the ability of the organization to be innovative.

Psychological Climate

Strategic Assumptions Analysis is a logical process for combining the experience and expertise of executives to produce better problem solutions. But the systematic integration of logic into any decision process is only half the story. The *psychological climate* of the environment in which discussions that lead to solutions take place is also critical to the successful flow of ideas. Recognition of the importance of this element in group processes has led to a number of systems to help break down interpersonal barriers and to "get the creative juices flowing." Examples of such processes are Synectics, developed by Arthur D. Little's research group (see Gordon [2]); TKG, a method widely used in Japan (Kobayashi [3]); and the Nominal Group Technique (Delbecq and Van de Ven [4]).

David Straus and Michael Doyle have analyzed how typical management meetings are held and have identified specific barriers to good decision making that are often created. Some of these barriers relate to the roles people are expected to assume in the meeting, others to the physical configuration of the meeting room itself. Doyle and Straus have developed the Interaction Method to overcome these problems.[5]

The Interaction Method centers on the designation and integration of three specific roles in meetings: the Chairman, the Facilitator, and the Recorder. Straus and Doyle are especially concerned with the role of the Chairman, which they say tends traditionally to be one of dominance. They propose instead that the Chairman be liberated from any role involving conflict so that he or she can indulge in a fair fight for strongly held ideas and points of view. This liberty, they say, is impossible given the clout inherent in the role of the Chairman as it is conventionally conceived. Most Chairmen are too important to their organizations to run their own meetings.

To counteract these tendencies, a neutral Facilitator helps to separate the Chairman's *process* role in the meeting from his or her *leadership* role in the company. The Chairman continues to open the meeting and evaluates the meeting's progress and procedures. Moreover, if collaboration and consensus building break down within the ranks, the Chairman can easily refit his or her authority mask. However, the procedural rules that govern the process of the meeting are the Facilitator's charge. When the agenda reaches an item that requires discussion and explication, the Facilitator assumes control of the meeting. This allows the Chairman to participate actively and aggressively in the meeting, and to advocate his or her projects. The Facilitator is responsible for making sure the participants are using the most effective methods for accomplishing their tasks in the shortest time, as well as for making group members stick to a common subject and a common process at all times. The Facilitator acts as a neutral police officer at the meeting to ensure that no one is allowed to dominate and that the group sticks to its task. The group has the right to remove any Facilitator who becomes overly dominant. Thus the Facilitator and the Chairman function as a team: The Facilitator makes sure the group members work together, and the Chairman ensures that the meeting agenda is clear, that realistic time limits have been established, and that organizational constraints are defined.

The role of the Recorder is also crucial to the Interaction

Method. His or her job is to serve as the "short-term memory" of the meeting by capturing the key ideas from discussions. The record should be plainly visible to all, so that, rather than asking participants to take notes on a pad of paper, it is best to have large sheets of paper taped to the walls of the meeting room. The Recorder's activity serves several key purposes. Most important, the group memory is a powerful visual aid that records the direction in which the meeting is flowing, assigns responsibility for follow-up, and eventually can act as the "agreement" among the group regarding what was decided or accomplished at the meeting. It also ensures that points made by a participant have been "heard" by the group, and it avoids wasting time by having to make repeated reference to previous points.

The design of the meeting room itself can have a significant impact on the success of a meeting. The typical rectangular or oval-shaped boardroom table creates an imbalance in group participation and thus a hindrance to creative problem solving. Such a scheme tends to encourage interactions back and forth across the table or, worse yet, toward the person at the end of the table, where, traditionally, the Chairman chooses to sit.

Circular meeting tables, although generally appropriate for informal discussions, have the opposite effect; that is, they don't readily provide participants a focal point from which issues can be led. In addition, if anger or aggression has developed within the group, this negative energy will be aimed directly at its target, and interpersonal confrontations can result.

Consequently, Doyle and Straus advocate a semicircular arrangement, such as the one illustrated in Figure 18. This scheme encourages all participants to break eye contact with colleagues, thus discouraging such emotion-charged encounters. It also enables everyone to focus attention on a common problem as it unfolds from the pen of the Recorder.

Optimal group decisions can emerge from a systematic,

Figure 18. Seating arrangement for optimal group decision making.

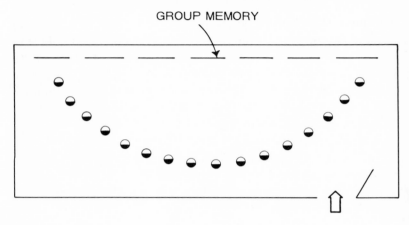

GROUP MEMORY

well-organized and -understood, facilitative working environment. Strategic Assumptions Analysis provides the foundation. Beliefs Assessment provides the judgmental technique
that enables decision makers to integrate their diverse
perspectives. And the Straus and Doyle Interaction Method
helps alleviate many of the organizational problems that
characterize many committee processes and undermine the
definition of effective solutions. In short, the success of such
processes doesn't happen by accident. It requires careful organization and detailed planning all the way down to the arrangement of the meeting room. Executives who have had
negative experiences in group sessions convened to address
business strategy should analyze whether adequate preparation went into the process before categorically rejecting this
approach. Teamwork is not always easy, but management
coparticipation in strategy design can produce powerful results.

Let's now turn our attention to yet another stumbling block
on the road to innovative decision making, one we examined
briefly in Chapter 3.

Improving the Roles of Management and Staff

Although staff groups usually have the time and training needed to conduct the sophisticated technical analyses that today's complex problem-solving techniques demand, these groups normally lack the fundamental information, experience, and perspectives to lead such investigations. We saw previously how the staff role differs from that of senior managers. Because they usually interact with an echelon of colleagues far removed from most staff members, executives have primary access to large amounts of data that are crucial to the organization's strategies, but that often don't filter down to the staff level. We also saw how the ineffective integration of staff into the decision-making process can result in a breakdown of the entire strategy effort.

Strategic Assumptions Analysis clarifies management and staff roles. Managers conduct the process. They formulate strategy options, develop and assess assumptions, agree on acceptable assumptions, and formulate the strategy most compatible with these beliefs. Managerial experience and judgment are "front stage" in Strategic Assumptions Analysis.

Although staff groups clearly perform a support role, their importance should not be understated. The Beliefs Assessment process provides a rich and quantifiable record of the bases on which key managerial assessments have been made. Many of these assessments, however, are made on incomplete information, and some are undoubtedly based on false perceptions. Staff groups can use such cases to establish their own analysis priorities for issues that need clarification. It is expected that the staff would report back to the managerial group with the findings of its research; by thus inducing managers to reconsider previous judgments, such work could have a major influence on strategy solutions. This system makes the cost-benefit assessment of staff contributions relatively easy. It all indicates strongly that little role confusion exists between management and staff.

Staff groups play a second critical role in Strategic Assumptions Analysis: They have responsibility for the method's information-tracking system. Continuous data collection and interpretation are critical to the long-term success of the overall process, for they provide the major inputs that lead to revisions of strategies over time. This is a relatively new role for staff people; SAA requires that they replace strategic data banks with strategic assumptions banks. These resources will require the collection of information relevant to the status of any assumption. The information must be analyzed by the staff groups and fed to managers whenever a significant change in an assumption's validity would affect the viability of enacted strategies.

The strategic information-tracking system illustrates how Strategic Assumptions Analysis deals with data. In Chapter 3, I made the case that data often get in the way of good strategy development, because managers depend too heavily on data to resolve issues of disagreement. Strategic Assumptions Analysis clearly alleviates this problem. The issue is resolved by using an interplay of strategies and assumptions to reach agreements; data simply help managers assess the various assumptions. Within the tracking system, however, data take on a new role. They become a critical part of a forward-oriented system to track assumptions validity. Data are thus collected for a specific well-defined purpose, and the cost justification of collecting various data can be established before the system is implemented. This orientation is significantly different from conventional strategic information, which focuses largely on capturing historical facts to provide nonspecific support for questions and issues that *might* arise in some future decision.

Chapter 3 also asked whether management objectives foster the best actions at all times. Strategic Assumptions Analysis forces this problem to the surface. How? The cost-of-error chart (Figure 12 in Chapter 4) clarifies the consequences of adopting one strategy position when nonoptimal assumptions might arise. By explicitly examining real and visible costs of these events, the decision-making group is forced to address the motivation and reward structure. When this is done, the problem will usually disappear, because factors that induce one to choose the "wrong" path can be addressed directly to the part of the organization that can best rectify the situation.

The success of Basic Materials in using Strategic Assumptions Analysis to redesign strategy for a venture that conformed to the company's traditional product line illustrates the method's effectiveness. But how does SAA stack up against other types of strategy problems? Let's take a look.

Launching Corporate New Business Programs

The track record of corporate efforts to launch new business programs in areas totally unrelated to their core activities has been less than spectacular. For this reason, most prefer the acquisition route to diversification.

The difficulties in starting a business from scratch are apparent to those companies that have attempted such undertakings. The initial problem is organizational. Naturally, a management team must be assembled. Usually the group comprises both insiders, who have the trust of senior management and have demonstrated their abilities to function effectively in the corporate system, as well as outsiders, who have specific knowledge and experience related to the business field of interest. Often the orientation and operating styles of these two groups are so dissimilar that internal friction develops. When that happens, most of the energies are devoted to resolving territorial and operating disputes, rather than actually addressing the problems of getting a new business launched.

Second, roadblocks can suddenly appear regarding corporate management's expectations from the business. Too often the venture is given a great deal of spending freedom early in the process with virtually no concern about turning a profit. But management subsequently expects the business to develop a proprietary market position that will lead quickly to market domination and large profits. The leap from one situation to the other rarely happens, and a crisis often results.

Aware of these looming pitfalls, the management team of a major energy company charged with developing a new business field decided to use Strategic Assumptions Analysis to formulate its plans. The corporation had earlier decided to develop a business in one of the high-potential alternative-energy-source areas (coal gasification, solar, nuclear). Energy Alternative Inc. (EAI), as we will call the group, assembled a team of six key managers (four of whom were recruited from the outside) and assigned a staff of about 50 professionals to tackle the problem.

Because the business area was not economically viable when the effort was launched, the managers faced a bewildering variety of issues that needed resolution:

- Should substantial R&D programs be established to accelerate technological developments?
- If so, should R&D be concentrated in one promising track, or should multiple routes be pursued?
- Should government funds be obtained to support the R&D effort?
- How much emphasis should be placed on acquisition?
- How much attention should be given to applications that are likely to become economically feasible in the short term versus the long term?
- Should a distribution network be established?

The group quickly realized that it was easier to pose questions than get answers.

The company's use of Strategic Assumptions Analysis was quite similar to that of the Basic Materials Super-Stuff venture group. But the significant particulars that arose at EAI in the factors that SAA emphasized and the impact that these elements had on the organization are worth highlighting.

From the very outset of the endeavor, the differences between the two companies became apparent. The managers at EAI lacked clearly defined alternative strategies, and no one "pounded the table" with strong conviction for a particular position. The managers were just as strong-willed as those at Basic Materials, but they lacked a corporate history in the area and so had fewer axes to grind for specific solutions.

Their lack of a historical perspective in the proposed new business and the fact that the core management group had only recently been assembled changed the emphasis of the process. Few of the managers knew very much about the perspectives and experiences of their associates. Strategic Assumptions Analysis provided the perfect problem-solving vehicle for them to gather their collective corporate knowledge and to integrate the various operating styles of team members. Through the SAA process, the core management group gained substantially greater cohesion. As an added benefit, the process gave the managers of Energy Alternative new insights into paths they might want to pursue in their own personal careers. Thus, the process served an important organizational development function for the fledgling business.

With respect to the specific strategy that was defined through SAA, the team identified its uncertainty over technological developments as the most critical issue to be resolved. It was apparent that EAI could not make bold commitments until the technology factors were clarified. More important, the group's management realized it didn't even know the current status of many key technological issues; hence forecasts of when and how breakthroughs might occur carried little credibility. As a result, the assumptions-tracking system became a far more important element in the plans than did any of the short-term strategy commitments that could be made.

Finally, members of Energy Alternative's strategy team discovered that their long-term success depended very much on getting corporate management to adopt specific postures with respect to capital investment in the new business. These postures were not necessarily compatible with overall corporate development philosophies. Therefore, the group launched a carefully designed program to orient corporate management to the new business and the factors that would affect success in it. The group was well aware that a disaster could erupt if the assumptions on which it based its decisions were not the same as the beliefs of top management.

The strategy priorities that EAI identified through Strategic Assumptions Analysis have now been converted into an operating plan. The management group is working in a unified and purposeful way. The team recognizes that its venture is risk-laden, but it believes it is in the maximum possible control of its future. To date, things are working well.

So far, I have illustrated Strategic Assumptions Analysis using cases in which major resources commitments were made to the process over a relatively long period of time. But the same philosophy can also be applied quickly to smaller problems. All that is required is the commitment to ask and answer important questions about the assumptions that underlie proposed solutions to problems. In the space of several hours, it is surprising how far one can progress in solving an apparent stalemate or in identifying new options to a "cut and dried" problem—as the following examples demonstrate.

Applying SAA to Operational Problems

Often, management consultants are called in to quell riots. It is an odd profession in many ways, thriving on crises and their companion sensationalized thrills. And spills. The consultant is not unlike the young Dutch boy whose technique with a faltering dike won him the unbridled acclaim of his compatriots—though had his thumb failed, the "riot" in compatriots would have been his undoing. A classic double bind.

I once was consulting for a company that was in the middle of one such crisis. At the start of the year its marketing department had forecast that sales of the key product group would decline over the next 12 months. As a result, the production department had shelved plans to expand capacity. Now, four months into the year and within three months of the season in which the product's sales would peak, sales were running 10 percent over the previous year's level and substantially over the original forecast. If the trend continued, there was no way the production capacity could satisfy the demand during the sales peak. The question: Should the company jump into a very expensive crash project to bring the additional capacity on stream right away?

The company's key marketing and production executives agreed to spend an afternoon in a strategy analysis session before making a final commitment. In the session, we quickly laid out the options and began to probe the major assumptions that supported each position. Almost immediately we perceived that the credibility of marketing forecasts was critical to the solution. However, a small investment in time exploring related but not so obvious assumptions revealed other solutions to the problem. It turned out that, although the marketing staff had a difficult time forecasting entry of new users into the category, it had considerable ability to manage demand through pricing policies. Furthermore, analysis showed that the short-term profit potential for the company was significantly higher by using price to regulate capacity–demand relationships than by trying to add capacity to meet all the potential sales. Thus, by going just one step beyond the obvious, we discovered new solutions that were superior to the options previously being debated.

A meeting structured around the principles of Strategic Assumptions Analysis also helped a large regional bank avoid a reorganization decision that was less than ideal. The bank was seeking ways to increase its business among small and medium-size companies. An analysis had shown that this sector was not well served either by the bank's corporate group, because these businesses were too small to receive much attention, or by the retail branch system, because business needs were different from the needs of individual customers. As a solution the bank was about to create a new independent unit to deal exclusively with the needs of this sector. The meeting was held to make one last assessment of the merits of the organizational change.

During the discussion of underlying assumptions related to strategy options, it became clear that the presence of a local branch was very important to the service needs of many of the target businesses. By organizationally separating the management of the branch from the development of business accounts, the bank ran a major risk of failing to be responsive to the market needs. The problem was solved by restructuring the proposed reorganization into a matrix form in which the branch service capabilities and the business account functions worked jointly on a day-to-day basis to structure programs that better met the needs of this sector.

Or consider the case of a pharmaceuticals company that faced a major pricing issue. The company had a branded prescription drug that dominated the market, but many states were promulgating legislation that favored having prescriptions filled with generic-equivalent products, if they were sold at a lower price. Should the company reduce its price to that of the generic-equivalent product in order to protect its sales? The company was leaning toward a partial price reduction, but not going all the way to the generic price. A quick assessment showed that this strategy was dominated by "either extreme"—that is, to maintain present pricing or meet generics head-on.

As the assumptions underlying the strategy options began to unfold, the company's management began to realize that the decision would have vast implications for the entire operating philosophy of the organization. The issue went to the heart of the company's ability to support new drug research. Consequently, the firm instituted a complete Strategic Assumptions Analysis of its problem in the broadest sense. As a result of this analysis, the pharmaceuticals company substantially reoriented its retailing policies, adopted new priorities in procurement, and instituted a complete review of the R&D system. The specific pricing decision became secondary to the much broader problem of which it was a part.

At this point, the reader may have the impression that Strategic Assumptions Analysis is being touted as a tool for all problems. It isn't. In fact, there is at least one major flaw in its use in business problems, as the next chapter points out.

REFERENCES

1. Saaty, T. L., "A Scaling Method for Priorities in Hierarchical Structures," *Journal of Mathematical Psychology*, June 1977, p. 243.

2. Gordon, W. J., *Synectics*. New York: Macmillan (1961).

3. Kobayashi, S., *Creative Management*. New York: American Management Associations (1971).

4. Delbecq, A. L., and A. H. Van de Ven, "A Group Process Model for Problem Identification and Program Planning," *Journal of Applied Behavioral Science*, 4: 1971.

5. Straus, D., and M. Doyle, "Making Board Meetings Work: The Doyle/Straus Interaction Method," *Directors and Boards*, Summer 1978, p. 4.

6

Stakeholder Management: Creating a More Cooperative External Environment

The consumer is not a moron. She is your wife. —DAVID OGILVY

Strategic Assumptions Analysis provides a disciplined managerial process for facilitating the formulation of creative corporate strategies. It is a means by which innovative solutions can be obtained to a wide variety of problems. But the process is flexible enough that it can be used for another purpose as well. We can literally use Strategic Assumptions Analysis on itself; that is, we can analyze the validity of the assumptions that are inherent in SAA as a problem-solving process.

Are SAA's own assumptions valid for all types of business problems? Unfortunately the answer is no. Let's see why.

SAA forces managers to examine all the assumptions that underlie a proposed strategy. By getting the subtle as well as the obvious assumptions out on the table early, there is a better chance that the strategy finally adopted will fit with the realities of the environment management expects to face. This is the heart of Strategic Assumptions Analysis. The most fundamental assumption underlying SAA is that the final strategy must be consistent with all key assumptions that management accepts as valid. Few would question this aspect of SAA. There are, however, two less obvious assumptions that are implicit in the process that will not be so readily accepted.

130

1. The assumptions that managers must make about the behavior of key stakeholders result in a sufficiently favorable environment for the company to achieve its objectives; that is, the best strategy that fits into the anticipated environment will produce acceptable results for
   the company.
2. The company cannot or ought not initiate special
   programs to change the behavior of key stakeholders in
   order to generate an external environment that will be
   more receptive to its strategies.

If these assumptions are not valid, then Strategic Assumptions
Analysis will produce disappointing results.

The Turbulent Business Environment

The Basic Materials case discussed in Chapter 4, for example,
illustrates options that do not surface under the SAA structure.
Remember that the "complete control" strategy critically depended on favorable resolution of proposed government regulation that could have eliminated the target beverage market
entirely. But the chances of such resolution were highly uncertain (see Figure 8). As a result, the final strategy was designed to reduce dependency on government agencies' behaviors. Was this the company's best strategy? That depends
on whether Basic Materials could have done anything to substantially lessen the chances that it would be regulated out of
the market. Success may have been possible, since effective,
far-sighted development of Super-Stuff might have quelled
many of the concerns that had led government officials to consider the new regulations. Although it would have required
substantially more technical development than was planned
for the "first generation" Super-Stuff beverage container,
management saw possibilities for the new container as an

energy source in municipal solid-waste-treatment centers after use as a one-way beverage container.

In this context, Super-Stuff might have possessed two functions simultaneously that would meet critical public needs: convenience container and energy source. But the risks of such sagacious initiatives would also have been high, because discussions with the government about the new product would also have alerted the company's competitors to the fledgling program. An analysis of this option would have been complex. The significance of all this, however, is that the issue of *altering* external conditions never even surfaced through Strategic Assumptions Analysis. Government behavior was treated as an uncontrollable condition which could affect the success of a Super-Stuff strategy, but not be affected by the strategy.

For a wide variety of corporate problems, Strategic Assumptions Analysis provides solutions that are well suited to the situation. There are, however, an increasing number of corporate issues for which it doesn't. This deficiency occurs most often in situations in which management faces an external environment so troublesome that any strategy it might logically adopt seems wholly unsatisfactory. The frustrations corporate executives experience in trying to deal with the four global issues presented in the first chapter—government regulation, employee motivation, technological innovation, and consumerist activities—often fall into this class. These issues are often so turbulent, and the behavior of key external groups so hostile, that nothing seems to work.

The situation seems to be deteriorating all the time. Consider the following accounts.

- In 1979, the federal government alone comprised 41 regulatory agencies, commanding a combined budget of over $4 billion. Business resources required to deal with these agencies are estimated to be over $100 billion.

- Congress is considering legislation that could greatly expand government's regulation of business practices. For example, the Human Resources Development Act would establish federal programs for experiments in worker-controlled plants.
- The Securities and Exchange Commission wants to give shareholders a greater voice in corporate policies, and has recently eased the restrictions on the addition of stockholder proposals in proxy material.
- Consumer groups grow stronger and become increasingly more sophisticated. Their use of the initiative to enact legislative change is certainly on the rise. California's Proposition 13 comes immediately to mind.
- Even the Better Business Bureau is getting into the act. The New York office of the Bureau recently expelled 15 companies with the scolding, "Good consumerism is good business."

The external constraints on how business operates continue to tighten. As this happens, the feasible space in which business can take appropriate action shrinks. Bold new thrusts to deal with strategic problems seem to become less and less viable. Even the maintenance of traditional products and markets cannot be taken for granted under the intensified pressures from external groups. Consider, for example, the recent plight of the cereal industry, the "heartland" companies that have produced products known and trusted by Americans for generations. These companies faced simultaneously a 1–2–3 punch from the external environment that threatened their very survival. First, the Federal Trade Commission attempted to split the four largest producers into smaller companies. Second, Action for Children's Television (ACT), a consumer group, is trying to ban advertisements for sugared cereals on children's television. And finally, the industry is being attacked from all sides for promoting foods with so-called "empty calories."

If the stakeholder environment becomes so constraining and hostile that one's survival is threatened, then Strategic Assumptions Analysis won't provide adequate solutions. In such dire straits, SAA can provide only answers whose conformances with the environment just aren't good enough. Under such conditions, only one option remains: Strategies must be implemented to *change* the organization's environment. Adaptation to it is patently unacceptable.

In recent years, many business leaders have recognized that they must become more active in shaping the external environment. They realize from painful experience that they can no longer constrain their activities to "the bottom line" management issues. They must don a more expansive spokesman's mask in the demanding dramas unfolding in society and politics. In short, they must become aggressive interventionists.

The commitment to alter the environment in which business operates is essential for fundamental change. But this role is a new and unfamiliar one for most executives. The challenge is enormous, and success will not come easily. For an indication of how difficult this undertaking is, let's take a look at what's been accomplished to date in an area that has received considerable support in business circles—advocacy advertising. The scorecard is not very encouraging.

Advocacy Advertising

Corporate spending on advocacy advertising rose dramatically during the 1970s. In 1971, corporate expenditures for major media nonproduct advertising exceeded $150 million; by 1978 this figure had swollen to more than $330 million. In addition, advertising by trade associations has risen more than 100 percent over the same period to nearly $150 million.[1] These figures substantially understate the actual spending levels, since they exclude newspapers, which represent a key medium for advocacy advertising.

The growth of advocacy advertising has been inspired by business concerns over the exploding regulatory role of the federal government and simultaneously over the slide of the public's confidence in business. Executives believe their views should be heard amid what they perceive as an avalanche of unwarranted criticism.

The approaches companies have taken to this issue have varied widely. Some have taken a broad perspective, highlighting threats to the free-enterprise system. Amway Home Products has taken this approach, specifically with a focus on government regulation. "Government used to be the referee," one Amway ad suggests. "Now it's the other team." Warner & Swasey has developed a campaign attacking U.S. foreign aid. Whirlpool ads address the issue of worker pride.

Advocacy advertising's most common strategy is to address issues that directly affect the company's businesses. Often this is done through trade associations. For example, Edison Electric Institute advocates nuclear power, the Savings & Loan Foundation wants tax breaks for interest on savings accounts, and the Tobacco Institute spokesmen call for more tolerance of smokers. Many companies are also taking advocacy positions directly on these issues. Aetna Insurance Company initiated a campaign advocating lower jury awards in corporate liability cases. SmithKline has begun an extensive campaign to address the issues surrounding excessively high drug costs and government regulation as a cause of inflationary prices.

But of all the organizations that are jumping on the advocacy advertising bandwagon, perhaps the most visible has been Mobil Oil Corporation. In 1978, Mobil spent $3.3 million on newspaper advocacy advertising. The company has been active in this area for years. In 1972 Mobil began running a series of full-page newspaper ads, warning that a natural gas crisis would occur unless government moderated its regulatory policies. When the crisis struck in 1975—just as Mobil had predicted—the company ran one last ad in frustration over the failure of government officials to heed Mobil's advice. The ad said essentially, "We told you so," and it included small-scale reproductions of previous ads.

In industry circles there is considerable disagreement as to the impact of Mobil's program. The company failed to obtain the policy changes it sought, at least concerning natural gas. But its visible posture may have helped convince the American people that the businessman's perspectives on major issues ought to be heard publicly. Presently the television networks will not permit advocacy advertising that they perceive as excessively controversial, a position that has been upheld by the U.S. Supreme Court. In a 1978 Opinion Research Corporation survey, 72 percent of the sample felt that corporations should be allowed to use television to present their views on controversial issues, and only 15 percent were opposed. (The remainder of respondents offered no opinion.)

A 1978 survey conducted by Yankelovich, Skelly & White and reported in the June 1978 issue of *Dun's Review* would lead one to question the effectiveness of Mobil's approach to advocacy advertising. When the public was asked which oil companies were "seriously concerned about doing something to solve the energy problem," only 9 percent named Mobil. This represented almost no improvement since 1974. During the same period other oil companies registered gains of up to 6 percent. Of the nine oil companies included in the survey, only one ranked lower than Mobil.

While Mobil's approach to advocacy advertising has received—at best—mixed reviews, the June 1979 issue of *Marketing and Media Decisions* reported that advocacy ads by the American Forest Institute were found to be quite effective. Fifty-six percent of government leaders and 70 percent of the public surveyed thought the ads were useful in supplying information on forestry issues.

Why did the Forest Institute's campaign succeed while Mobil's failed? James Plumb, who was in charge of the Forest Institute campaign, claimed that tests had shown that the more argumentative the advertising, the less convincing it became. In his opinion, the most effective ads state an industry's position, but don't explicitly argue on its behalf.

In the same article, John O'Toole, president of the ad agency Foote, Cone & Belding, echoed Plumb's thoughts but took them a step further. O'Toole argued that corporate advocacy advertising can be effective only if the ad addresses the consumer's problems, rather than arguing the company's point of view.

I believe that O'Toole's analysis gets to the heart of the issue. Advocacy advertising is communication between an organization and its constituents. Such advertising provides information in the hope of motivating its audience to specific actions. In this respect, it has the same objective that product advertising has in trying to influence consumer purchase decisions. Product advertising is most effective when it talks the consumer's language and shows the benefits to the buyer of purchasing the company's brand. Product advertising does not discuss the benefits the company will realize if the consumer does what the ad asks. Why should advocacy advertising not work in the same way?

Most advocacy advertising comes up short on articulating constituency benefits. Usually, the problem is far more fundamental than merely insensitive ad copy. Rather, it is the failure of the company to realize that an advocacy campaign's success depends on its ability to create a closer partnership between the corporation and its constituents. Too many companies treat the problem as part of a public relations function. Normally, the objective is merely to "get the message out." The communication turns out to be nonreciprocating: Changes in company policies are not considered to be a viable strategy option. Too often the effort resembles a man with earplugs and a bullhorn on the steps of corporate headquarters shouting, "You don't understand my problems!"

A conscientious effort to improve the environment in which

a company operates must be undertaken as an organization-wide strategy. The plan involves the *actions* the company takes as much as or more than what is said. This implies that the entire cadre of top managers must be integrally tied to the effort, not just the public relations group. It also means that the company's profit-oriented operating policies must be integrated with its external strategies. In short, the effort involves a top-to-bottom change in management processes and management philosophies. *Stakeholder Management* was designed as one possible framework for meeting these often formidable challenges.

A Stakeholder Framework for Business

Traditionally, a company's stockholders have been viewed as having ultimate external control over the policies and practices that management adopts in running the business. Such positional power is based on the stockholder's financial stake in the company's profits. Although this group continues to influence management actions, many other external groups exist that also exercise control over the corporation's policies. Each such group believes it has a legitimate *stake* in the corporation, and each may evaluate corporate actions in a different way. It is precisely these diverse and often conflicting external pressures that make effective, comprehensive stakeholder management so elusive.

We use the term *stakeholder* to identify the various pressure groups a corporation must address. The concept has been used previously in conjunction with Strategic Assumptions Analysis. Here the stakeholder notion will be more fully developed to refer to any group whose collective behavior can explicitly affect the organization's future, but over which the organization has little, if any, direct control—for example, suppliers, customers, owners, employees, competitors, trade associations, special-interest groups, and government organizations. The exact nature and number of stakeholders will depend on the characteristics of the particular organization.

Nearly all corporate executives recognize—all too painfully for some—the problems I'm addressing. Early in 1979, *Business Week* [2] devoted a major article to these issues. The cover illustration synthesized things perfectly; it showed a corporate castle besieged by consumerists, environmentalists, regulatory bodies, and other interest groups. The story was laced with executives' quotes attesting to the fact that the rules of the game have shifted, often requiring radical changes in the thrust of their public relations activities. But *Business Week* provided little in the way of concrete solutions to the mounting crunch from external forces that most executives are experiencing. That's because there are no generally accepted ways of handling the entire problem as one management issue.

While most organizations have some way of dealing with many of their stakeholder groups, they usually do so in a fragmented way by concentrating on one or two stakeholders and ignoring or putting minimal resources against the rest. Issues such as ensuring that raw-materials shortages do not reoccur, forming strategies for dealing with proposed government energy policies, conducting employee wage-benefit negotiations, and creating a marketing campaign for a new product line are all on the executive slate at the same time. Managers normally handle these issues on a case-by-case basis, allotting to them attention proportional to the current leverage the stakeholder has over the organization.

It isn't enough to acknowledge that, in the face of surging external pressures, strategy building is a new ball game. Nor can we claim that revitalized, slick PR will effectively deal with these forces; the performance of the widely used—often abused—advocacy advertising has been less than spectacular. Nor is it adequate to assert that executives ought to develop an integrated perspective for addressing stakeholder issues. There must also be concrete *managerial processes* that turn philosophies and concepts into actions—into offensive business tactics.

The stakeholder approach meets these issues head-on and facilitates a number of key management activities. First, it enables managers to identify priorities and assign them systematically to their organizations' objectives. Second, it forces managers to explicitly recognize all the diverse groups that claim to have a stake in the organization. By drawing stakeholder maps, such as the one illustrated in Figure 19, executives become conscious of *all* the external pressures they face, not just those that happen to be visible at a particular time. Third, stakeholder management encourages the par-

Figure 19. Stakeholder map.

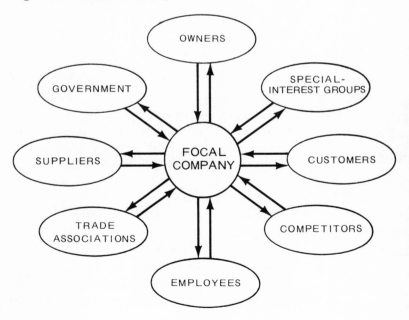

ticipative input of a wide range of key executives whose varied experiences with different stakeholders provide the company with insights essential to making good strategies. Finally, the stakeholder framework enables executives to develop fresh perspectives on stakeholder behaviors, which can be translated into day-to-day tactics for managing corporate relations with these groups.

The stakeholder management process will be introduced using external relations issues as the focus because this represents the single most significant area of application. However, the principles apply equally to problems within the corporation, in which case the stakeholders are identified as other organizational units. The battle to get change instituted within the corporation can be just as difficult as and can require just as much strategy as the battle to resolve external issues. The inside-oriented application of the process will be discussed later in the chapter.

Two basic principles underlie the Stakeholder Management framework:

1. The central goal is to achieve maximum overall cooperation between the entire system of stakeholder groups and the objectives of the corporation (that is, the behavior of all groups is maximally supportive of the objectives).
2. The most efficient and effective strategies for managing stakeholder relations involve efforts that deal simultaneously with issues affecting multiple stakeholders.

The health of an organization in a stakeholder sense is analogous to human health in a biological sense: Unless all organs of the body are functioning satisfactorily, the overall system cannot function effectively. We believe that the organization can take actions equivalent to diet control and exercise to maintain proper balance on a number of fronts. The failure of most corporations to develop effective strategies for dealing with stakeholders is indicative of the fact that a systematic stakeholder framework for managing the external environment is not normally utilized.

Besides treating stakeholder management issues systematically, organizations must recognize that they cannot confine their efforts to direct, immediate stakeholders. Figure 19 is actually a simplification of the typical relationship between a corporation and its stakeholders. The situation normally looks more like the network depicted in Figure 20.

To illustrate this intensified complexity, consider the recent efforts of the National Organization for Women (NOW) to gain passage of the Equal Rights Amendment (ERA). Using the

Figure 20.   Real-world stakeholder map.

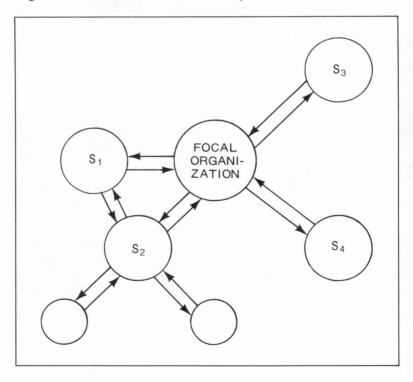

notation of Figure 20, assume (1) the Focal Organization is the state legislature in a state that has not passed ERA; (2) S_1 is the business community, which chooses cities for large conventions and, through these decisions, has a significant cascade effect on the financial revenues of cities so chosen; and (3) S_2 is NOW. NOW has had direct, but limited, influence on the state legislatures to pass ERA. However, by pressuring businesses to boycott convention cities in states that have not passed ERA, NOW has exerted enormous indirect pressure on those states' legislatures. This indirect strategy has had a tremendous impact. It is estimated that, as of 1978, Chicago had lost $15 million, Atlanta $6 million, and Miami $4.5 million because of the boycott. The effect of this strategy was just what NOW had wanted—Kansas City filed suit against the Missouri legislature asking for damages and demanding passage of the amendment.

The use of third-party coalitions—whether or not the third party supports the strategy—can be a powerful vehicle for managing external stakeholder relations. Stakeholder Management has been designed to help business identify and use the best resources to create a more favorable environment.

As of this writing the process has been tested on specific stakeholder problems in several corporations. Some of these results will be described shortly. But the process has not been in existence long enough to obtain long-term results of implementing the total process as a continuing management philosophy.

Since we don't have many actual Stakeholder Management case histories to draw on, the best method for providing an overall feeling for the process as it applies to real business problems is "postmortem" analysis; that is, to retrospectively apply the Stakeholder Management decision framework to a problem that has already unfolded. Needless to say, Monday-morning quarterbacking is infinitely easier than making decisions under real-world constraints. But if we keep this disclaimer in mind, a postmortem analysis of an actual case history can provide valuable insights. We'll examine a case with which I am personally familiar—the issue of government regulation of all beer and soft-drink containers, either through taxation or by requiring that all such containers be returnable.

My brief characterization of what actually occurred or what might have happened in certain critical stages of the issue's development and its solution is necessarily a simplification of complex events. A more complete treatment has been published elsewhere.[3] As the case unfolds, the reader will recognize that the timing of the beverage container issue and its relevance to possible strategies Basic Materials could employ for its Super-Stuff product introduction had strong implications for the company's planning in 1977. But the coincidence of these two events is by no means exceptional. That corporate strategy considerations are so closely tied to developments in the external environment—here in the regulatory arena— represents very accurately the dilemma in which most businesses find themselves today.

The group that organized and coordinated the beverage industry's strategy for dealing with the container issue was the United States Brewers Association (USBA). During the late sixties and early seventies, Henry King, president of the USBA, had spent enormous amounts of his own and his staff's time and energy on the problem. The issues King faced were certainly not straightforward, and the choices confronting him and his colleagues were anything but clear. Given these obstacles, the USBA's effort to shape the industry's strategy for dealing with the container issue was superb. Let's look at the sequence of events as they started to develop in the late sixties.

The Returnable-Container Strategy

The War/Woodstock/Watergate era of the late 1960s and early 1970s is marked by heightened social consciousness and calls for change on many fronts—most notably in institutions—much of it positive, some of it merely humankind's need for a rallying cause. With the emergence of highly vocal consumer and environmentalist groups came demands that business act more responsibly, for example, in doing its part to improve the quality of the nation's ecological system. Many groups spotlighted container litter—much of it nonbiodegradable—as a salient contributor to environmental pollution. A strong attack against beverage containers materialized from another angle as well: Even if properly disposed of, containers represent an unnecessary waste of scarce resources. The "Ban the Can" movement was thus born.

In light of this call for a constructive solution to this issue, the U.S. beverage container industry found itself confronted with what it believed to be a limited set of appropriate responses: Force distribution of the returnable bottle as the sole source of beverage packaging, or continue with the present system of using both one-ways and returnables.

Early in the controversy, the issues were debated before a number of state and local legislatures. Bills to restrict or eliminate returnable containers were proposed with backing from consumer and environmentalist groups. Although many such initiatives were made, the industry's arguments, which centered on the economic practicality of the existing system, persuaded almost all the legislative bodies to reject the reform proposals. The major exceptions were Oregon and Vermont, which in 1972 passed laws that required minimum deposits on all beer and soft-drink containers, and Washington, which in 1973 passed a law placing a tax of $.005 on each beer and soft-drink container, the proceeds to be used for litter cleanup programs.

The USBA is the nation's oldest trade association, formed in 1862 to assist in ensuring compliance with a government tax on beer. Over the years its role has expanded to keep pace with the growing government regulation of the entire beverage industry. As a result, membership in the Association grew to include not only brewers but also the manufacturers and suppliers of beverage containers and the major soft-drink manufacturers. Thus the USBA was the natural group to carry the industry's banner into the brawl over the container issue.

The industry was, of course, against regulatory or legislative restrictions on beverage packaging. It wanted the marketplace to determine which beverage containers would exist. Its strategy to deal with the threat was simple: Marshal the facts about the economic harm such imposed change would create, and develop a strong industry and labor coalition to back the position.

Until 1976 the strategy worked almost flawlessly. But then the rules of the game changed. Four states—Maine, Michigan, Massachusetts, and Colorado—placed proposed beverage container legislation on the ballot for the voters to decide directly as a referendum issue. Now the general population, not the legislatures, would make the decisions.

In retrospect, the USBA strategists underestimated the significance of this shift. Once again they trotted out their tried-and-true arguments about economic costs. They pressed their message through a mass-media blitz in each state just prior to its referendum. But this time the tactic didn't work. Maine and Michigan passed laws to restrict one-way containers, and Massachusetts narrowly defeated the proposed change.

These two devastating defeats caught the industry completely off guard. A crash program was initiated to identify what went wrong. Henry King made this assessment publicly following the study:

> We've reconfirmed that litter is the problem—that the public really cares little about other issues. While some brewers question the validity of the study, most don't. One study found that our advertising may have been counterproductive, particularly with themes of jobs and costs. The theme that deposit legislation won't do the job is the theme that works best. Our advertising was perceived to be self-serving.[4]

The results of the study provided an explanation of why Colorado was the only state to defeat the proposed change decisively. Of the four target states, Colorado alone had an organized recycling program for aluminum containers. Thus Colorado voters had envisioned other options to "ban the can" initiatives.

The industry coalition was shaken to the core. Members began operating independently. For example, Alcoa Aluminum initiated a national advertising campaign to promote recycling of aluminum cans. The theme "We can't wait" thus took on a double meaning. Brewers began to take open, though reactionary, actions that served their own interests. Tensions rose, and in 1969 Miller, the second-largest brewer, withdrew from the USBA. In the same year Connecticut passed legislation to restrict the use of one-way beverage containers. Proposals for such restrictions in other states and localities have also accelerated significantly since 1976.

The story hasn't yet ended, but the prospects for the industry aren't bright. Could this debacle have been avoided by employing an alternative management system, such as a stakeholder framework? No one can say for sure. But let's consider how Stakeholder Management *could* have flagged issues that were not considered.

Stakeholder Management and the Container Issue

As Figure 21 illustrates, Stakeholder Management comprises five distinct phases. The process is continuous in the sense that the results of the fifth phase loop backward to provide a reassessment of the issues in the first phase. This implies that Stakeholder Management is an ongoing process designed to affect long-term corporate management of the external environment; it is not a one-shot problem-solving technique that can be turned on or off depending on problems that surface at

Figure 21. The Stakeholder Management process.

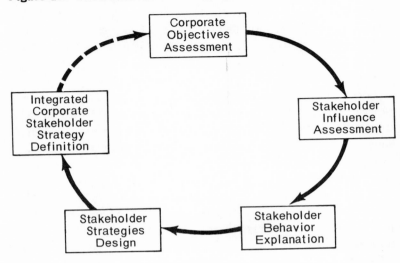

a particular time. We shall select a few key points in each of the five phases of the process to illustrate how Stakeholder Management helps to expand and enrich strategic options.

Phase 1. Assess Corporate Objectives

Given the complexity of managing the external environment, the maxim "Know thyself" is a good place to start. The goal of Stakeholder Management is to keep the behavioral patterns of stakeholders in balanced cooperation with the organization's fundamental purposes. Therefore, management must first clearly define the organization's objectives and assess the relative importance of achieving each of them.

In trying to solve the container problem, the USBA was implicitly also trying to meet its objectives as a trade association. These sets of objectives are not necessarily compatible, however. For example, solutions that are best for the brewers are not necessarily best for container manufacturers or the soft-drink companies. How much emphasis should be placed on serving each of the Association's constituents? Even within a constituency, solutions may benefit some groups more than others. For instance, large brewers have a different perspective from that of small ones. What emphasis should the Association place on serving individual brewers?

Objectives setting is neither a new nor an especially difficult task for executives. Many techniques exist for turning corporate philosophy, style, and generic purposes into specific operational objectives. It is important, however, that the technique be process oriented and that it encourage interaction and consensus. If you adopt an objectives-setting technique that ignores these factors, either you will drastically undermine support for your objectives, or you will come up with an objective that, like motherhood and apple pie, pleases everybody but means nothing.

For example, it was easy for the USBA to ignore the tradeoffs of highly volatile strategies with statements like, "Our primary objective is to serve all our members." But this posture turned out to be a fatal trap, because the Association found that the *only* position it could take was, "The status quo is best," because that avoided the issue. Such a position may not directly hurt any constituency, but neither will it necessarily help. This restrained outlook nearly guarantees that the organization will not be capable of initiating required changes and will ultimately lose its power. There is some evidence that the USBA found itself in precisely this dilemma as the events of the container issue unfolded.

Assessing the relative importance of objectives is a vital part of stakeholder analysis, because these priorities determine the axes of cooperation or conflict that may develop with various stakeholders. Objectives themselves often create "love/hate" relationships with stakeholders as companies try to pursue mutually incompatible purposes. One major company with a dominant share position in its primary market recently sought to further expand its share—at the same time it was fighting antitrust suits for ruthlessness against its competition. A group of hospital administrators wrestled with the conflict of introducing cost-cutting efficiency measures while trying to upgrade the effectiveness of medical care.

The USBA faced the dilemma of either losing some of its members by taking an active stance on the container issue or protecting the membership coalition by sitting pat. The tradeoff of priorities to objectives cannot be avoided if the external environment is to be effectively managed. The issues must be laid out on the table, and the hard choices must be faced directly if the program is to have a chance of succeeding.

Beliefs Assessment, described in Chapter 5 in conjunction with Strategic Assumptions Analysis, is perfectly suited to identifying priorities of objectives. It encourages rich discussions among executives around their reasons for emphasizing one goal over another. During the course of discussions, motherhood objectives such as "We want to turn a profit" or "Our goal is to possess industry dominance" become frivolous, and they are often restructured or removed. The primary value of this activity, however, lies in developing a common perspective among executives as to where the organization ought to be headed.

Phase 2. Assess Stakeholder Influence

Once managers have reached consensus on priorities for objectives, their next task is to assess the influence of their various stakeholders according to these objectives. First, managers must identify the company's stakeholders. This is accomplished by asking, "Which groups or organizations, over which the corporation has no direct control, can directly affect the achievement of corporate objectives?" At least 11 major stakeholders were relevant to the USBA's container strategy: can manufacturers, bottle manufacturers, retailers, soft-drink manufacturers, brewers, labor organizations, the Environmental Protection Agency, the U.S. Department of Energy, environmentalists, state government officials, and voters.

The specific impact of each stakeholder's behavior on each objective must then be identified. This assessment avoids the problem of devising strategies for dealing with stakeholders based on generalities. Rather than ask whether, for example, the EPA is "for us" or "against us," the process forces an answer to the question, "What actions or behaviors can the agency take to undermine our objectives, and what can they do to help us achieve these goals?" This question must be asked for each objective, because the answers may be very different depending on which objective is being considered. For example, doctors are in total agreement with hospital decisions to add new equipment that will improve patient care, but normally they are very hostile toward moves to cut costs.

In analyzing stakeholder influence, three sets of behaviors must be identified for each stakeholder: (1) *actual behavior*—what a stakeholder is currently doing to affect a corporation's achievement of its objectives; (2) *cooperative potential*—actions a stakeholder could potentially take to help the corporation achieve its objectives; and (3) *competitive threat*—what a stakeholder could potentially do to prevent the corporation from achieving its objectives. Throughout the discussion of the stakeholder management process, I will use the terms "cooperative" and "competitive" to describe stakeholder postures. These terms are used with quite specific definitions. They describe the degree to which the stakeholder's behavior helps or hinders a company's achievement of its objectives. Thus the concepts are opposite points on the same scale, similar to "boiling" and "freezing," which describe the temperature of water. There should be no confusion between minimizing competition as a stakeholder objective and the necessity of competition as a fundamental characteristic of the free market system. Marketplace competition forces companies to differentiate their products and services, which in turn minimizes the type of competition being used in the stakeholder structure. The two senses of the term competition are very compatible.

In analyzing stakeholder behaviors, many executives get trapped by considering too narrow a range of stakeholder actions. They try merely to neutralize traditional rivals instead of making them cooperative partners, and they seldom worry about losing friends. One public utility that seriously considered the range of possible behaviors of a traditionally hostile rate commission discovered that a great deal more cooperative potential existed than it had first assumed. Traditional "enemies" can become friends, but this metamorphosis requires that one believe that such reconciliations are at least possible.

A similar opportunity that is often ignored without a systematic assessment of stakeholder influence is the mobilization of groups that are currently neutral and inactive. Many organizations have discovered that legislative changes that are hopelessly deadlocked can be unblocked by mobilizing voters through the initiative process. Company employees, who are often treated as a passive and uninvolved group in resolving key corporate issues, can become a major force in turning the tide one way or the other.

Let us briefly examine the actual, cooperative, and competitive behaviors of a couple of key stakeholders in the USBA's environment. First, consider the behavior of the can manufacturers. What was their actual behavior just prior to the 1976 referenda votes? This group fully supported the industry position that restrictions on nonreturnable containers would be economically disastrous. The aluminum manufacturers were also investing in recycling capabilities in those areas of the country in which the aluminum package held substantial market shares. Most can manufacturers were also diversifying into new businesses, while investment in new can-making facilities was slowing down.

The cooperative potential and the competitive threat of the can manufacturers relate to a single question: How strong is their commitment to the future of the beverage can business?

Cooperative behavior would involve major research-and-development spending on new technologies to reduce can costs (by requiring less energy) and to make them more ecologically desirable (by making them biodegradable). The companies could also reduce profit margins on cans to enhance the argument addressing the economic penalties of moving to an all-returnable system. If the can manufacturers moved to their competitive threat, they would treat the beverage container business as a "cash cow." Margins would be increased to the limit and short-term profits would be used to acquire or build alternative businesses. Obviously this posture would erode the industry's basic economic argument in defending maintenance of nonreturnable containers.

To see how the behaviors of the various stakeholders interact, let's look briefly at the posture of the brewers. The actual behavior of this group included strong public support for a nonreturnable system. But the brewers were also in the process of implementing an aggressive program of vertical integration into the self-manufacture of cans. In one sense this action reinforced their commitment to the viability of nonreturnable containers, but it also had a clear effect on the posture of the can manufacturers.

As a stakeholder group, the brewers' actual behavior was nearly at its cooperative potential. In terms of the beverage industry, however, the vertical integration strategy may have caused overall deterioration of this group's support. This will be explicitly considered when USBA strategies are examined in a later phase of the analysis.

The competitive threat of the brewers is rather extensive. In 1976, no brewer was taking unilateral action; all supported maintaining the status quo. But the brewers did not face equal levels of risk if the system were forced to change. Coors, for example, had a lot to lose. The company was committed to aluminum cans, both because of its vertical integration into that technology and because of the large geographic area served by its sole brewery. Other brewers, particularly some of the smaller regional firms, might even have benefited from an all-returnable-container system. The threat of unilateral actions by brewers was significant, and the damage it could have done to the industry coalition was enormous.

Once actual behavior, cooperative potential, and competitive threat are defined for each stakeholder, the process provides a picture of the possible influence each stakeholder has on the corporation. In order to assess the importance of a stakeholder's influence, two judgments must be made: (1) the relative worth of inducing a stakeholder to move from its present behavior to its cooperative potential, and (2) the relative harm of allowing a stakeholder to move to its competitive threat. The relative cooperation of stakeholders requires an answer to the question, "How much better off would the corporation be if Stakeholder A rather than Stakeholder B were to become cooperative?" By answering this question for cooperative and competitive behaviors of stakeholders relative to each objective, one can assess both the positive and the negative potentials of a stakeholder. Once again, the Beliefs Assessment technique can be used to facilitate these judgments.

When the judgments of cooperative and competitive stakeholder potentials have been developed for each objective, the importance weighting of each objective can be used to develop an overall index of stakeholder cooperative and competitive potential. From this index we can develop a map such as the one illustrated in Figure 22. These maps enable the company to single out a group of stakeholders as targets for further analysis.

For example, executives may identify 15 stakeholders. After listing their individual behaviors and ranking the relative importance of each, the executives may find that three stakeholders have high cooperative potentials and four have high

Figure 22. Map of stakeholder potentials.

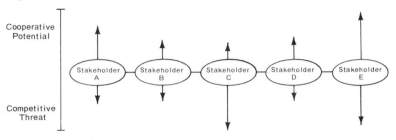

competitive threats. The executives must now make a decision on where to concentrate their resources. If they wish to minimize the deterioration of the stakeholder environment, they may choose to work on strategies for the four negative stakeholders. Or, if they wish to try to maximize cooperation, they may concentrate on the three positive stakeholders. Or they may wish to combine both factors and deal with the stakeholders that have the greatest overall impact. Regardless of their decision, at the end of this phase the executives should have a much better feel for how different stakeholders can affect their organization's future.

Phase 3. Explain Stakeholder Behaviors

By the end of Phase 2, a clear picture should emerge of the corporation's specific objectives and the impact that stakeholders' actual and potential behaviors can have on the attainment of these goals. But if managers are to generate meaningful strategic options, they must first understand why a particular stakeholder would act in a certain way. What would induce a group to behave cooperatively? Competitively? Such an analysis yields two benefits.

- First, it provides an understanding of a stakeholder's actual behavior—his needs and his beliefs about other stakeholders.

- Second, it provides an understanding of what the world would have to be like to induce a stakeholder to become either cooperative or competitive.

The most important requirement for understanding a stakeholder's behavior is the perception of its objectives. Gaining insight into this realm, however, is not a simple matter. For example, expensive and sophisticated market research procedures are often used in an attempt to identify consumer purchasing objectives. Even with such massive efforts, companies often produce products and services that consumers reject because they don't meet their needs.

Let's examine the causes of behavior patterns for the most central stakeholder in the container issue—the voter. Collectively, the voting public was confused about the ramifications of the container legislation. In all four states, the voters remained undecided about their position for most of the preelection discussions.

What would swing the voters' sentiments in one direction or another? Clearly, voting decisions are ultimately based on beliefs about how well the current or the proposed system will meet the public's objectives. The USBA's research confirmed that two voter objectives overrode all others: reduction of litter and obtaining beverages at reasonable cost. The core of the industry's argument was developed from an economic base, primarily because the industry knew those issues best. Using economic arguments, the Association showed that eliminating one-way containers would raise prices, cost skilled jobs, and disrupt distribution systems. This strategy assumed implicitly that nearly all the voters' concerns centered on the second objective. However, as indicated earlier, the voters were most concerned about litter, a problem the industry campaigns ignored. The fallacy of the economic argument can easily be seen by considering the fact that the economic assumption is directly relevant only to voters who buy beer or soft drinks.

Clearly the weight of importance of this objective is related to the quantity of beverages a voter consumes. The USBA's misperception of the key issue was the major reason its argument failed in half the states in which referenda were held.

The identification of stakeholder objectives completes half of the explanation of behaviors. The other half is identifying why the stakeholders believe their behaviors are the best way to achieve their objectives. These reasons are often related to the stakeholder's own perceptions of his or her particular stakeholder environment, perhaps even including the actions of the organization conducting the analysis.

Given voters' objectives, what will tip the balance in favor of one solution or another? The key factor is the relative credibility of the beverage industry and the government positions in the eyes of the consumer. Rejection of container restrictions is more likely if a voter believes (1) the beverage industry can effectively solve the problem if left to itself; and/or (2) there is too much government interference in the marketplace already, and the proposed solutions will only raise prices without solving the litter problem. On the other hand, a voter is likely to favor the legislative change if he or she believes (1) the beverage industry arguments are self-serving and responsive only to company profit goals, rather than consumers' problems; and/or (2) the government proposals are the only viable solutions to the litter issue.

For example, Colorado voters soundly defeated the proposed legislation because they felt it was simply the wrong solution. Colorado has maintained an active program of recycling aluminum cans for years, and this was felt to offer a greater long-range potential solution to the problem of litter and waste of resources. The two states that passed the referenda were both in areas in which little or no recycling takes place. Shortly after the 1976 results, Alcoa began the aforementioned national advocacy campaign to encourage aluminum-can recycling with the theme, "We can't wait."

The explanation of stakeholder behavior should be summarizable as a statement such as: "Stakeholder S has chosen Behavior B to achieve Objective O for Reason R." It should be emphasized that the analysis that produces this explanation represents the beliefs of the organization conducting the analysis, rather than the facts about the stakeholder. As such, the degree of certainty about the beliefs should be assessed before the organization proceeds to the next stage of the process. If a high degree of uncertainty exists, research should be initiated to clarify positions. Otherwise, strategies will be built on a sand foundation. And as we know, sand foundations are doomed to crumble.

Phase 4. Design Stakeholder Strategies

The first three stages of the stakeholder analysis process complete the organization's initial attempt at understanding pressures from the external environment. At this point in the analysis, executives have identified their own objectives and assessed how each stakeholder can affect them. These executives have also developed an analysis of the motivations and desires of each target stakeholder and the reasons for its behavior. The strategy design phase builds on the foundation of knowledge from these earlier phases. It focuses on trying to increase the chances of cooperative behavior for each target stakeholder or, alternatively, on trying to decrease the chances of competitive behavior. For each stakeholder, there is one of two ways to proceed.

The first technique of strategy design is to identify direct-strategy options. A direct strategy is one in which the organization tries to increase the chances of more cooperative behavior and/or reduce the chances of competitive behavior by dealing directly with the stakeholder whose behavior the organization is trying to change. Simply providing information to the stakeholder is one example of a direct strategy. Or, using the explanatory analysis of Phase 3, the organization can inform the stakeholder of other options.

Perhaps the stakeholder is simply ignorant of a win–win strategy and would be willing to move to such a strategy once aware of it. Information about the organization and the stakeholder relationship is the critical issue here. In addition to providing options to the stakeholder, the organization can increase the attractiveness of more cooperative actions by introducing new inducements to choose the alternative. As a last resort, the organization can try to motivate the stakeholder to change its objectives by some direct action. The legal constraints on this kind of direct-strategy option, which consists of "Mafia tactics" in the extreme (that is, giving the stakeholder an offer it can't refuse), can complicate its implementation.

Many companies unknowingly block cooperative actions by stakeholders because they are insensitive to stakeholders' objectives. Executives who have tried to introduce job enrichment programs and worker participation have often witnessed actions by union leaders that sabotage such programs. The changes may be beneficial to the workforce, but if they threaten the union's survival in any way, clearly they will be resisted. A little planning and negotiation with those issues in mind can make a tremendous difference in the outcome.

Sometimes there are natural opportunities to reorient the objectives of stakeholders without manipulative controls or underhanded tactics. Simply offering the opportunity of meaningful corporate career opportunities to women who are now channeling their efforts into the consumerist movement might help them redirect pent-up energies along more cooperative avenues. By not being offered choices, these groups see their objectives as unnecessarily constrained, which makes them a threat to the company.

In the USBA's case, its advocacy advertising campaign in the four states that faced referenda was a direct strategy the Association undertook to try to ease the voters into a more cooperative frame of mind. The advertising stressed jobs, energy, and costs, and it pointed in these terms to the economic consequences of moving to an all-returnable-container system. Thus, in our terms, the USBA was trying to increase the attractiveness of a cooperative behavior—voting "no" on container legislation—by offering new reasons to voters to vote "no." Unfortunately, this strategy failed, because the USBA was acting on a misperception of voters' true concerns and objectives.

The second technique in strategy design is to use the explanatory analysis to generate indirect-strategy options, those in which third parties are used to motivate behavioral change in the stakeholder. The NOW boycott cited earlier in the chapter is an indirect, third-party strategy. Such strategy options, however, are not always obvious. They may require working through a stakeholder group that was initially believed to be unimportant. This step may force the organization to choose new target stakeholders through whom the organization wants to work, and to explain their behaviors.

To illustrate this phase of the Stakeholder Management process, let's examine several direct- and indirect-strategy options for dealing with a few of the key stakeholders.

CAN MANUFACTURERS

In order to increase the cooperative behavior of the can manufacturers—that is, to get them to commit more heavily to can manufacturing—the USBA needs to convince manufacturers that the can business has long-term growth potential. One possible strategy is for the Association to try to get the brewers to stop their vertical integration and leave the can-making business to the can manufacturers. Tricky antitrust problems complicate this strategy, but if it worked it would provide the can manufacturers with an incentive to stop their diversification program. An alternative would be to get the brewers to invest in new can research, as a signal that the brewers are strongly committed to metal cans. In addition, the USBA needs to convince the manufacturers that the USBA's economic argument is effective.

BREWERS

The strategy for the brewers must ensure that this group remains committed to the coalition the USBA has built, and that its members do not go their separate ways on the container issue. The driving force behind this strategy may well involve economic arguments and continued emphasis on the potentially disastrous effects of any container legislation. Tied to this argument must be a statement that the brewers can work effectively only through a coalition, and further, that some short-term losses in localities and states can be made up by delaying legislation as long as possible.

ENVIRONMENTALISTS

Though there may be little to be done to make this rather hostile group more cooperative, in the case of environmentalists the USBA is in a virtual no-risk situation. To the extent that the environmentalists are already as competitive as possible, a radical strategy may be in order here. Since environmentalists are ultimately concerned with the quality of the environment, perhaps the USBA could propose antipollution programs for the industry, or try to take the "leading edge" across a number of industries in pollution control. Such a strategy could induce the environmentalists to adopt a less hostile posture, and it could put the USBA into more of a negotiative position for the future.

VOTERS

The voters' true concern is litter. Hence, an advertising campaign that recognizes the problem and promotes what the USBA (or its represented industries) is doing about the litter problem would be effective. The campaign should emphasize that mandatory deposits on all containers will not answer the problem. However, a campaign that is entirely "negative" will be seen as self-serving. Such a strategy is precisely what the USBA has argued it should have done (see earlier quote from

Henry King). The implementation of this strategy is tricky, because it may carry some risk of alienating labor without the proper precautions. That is, the USBA must assure labor that it is truly concerned about the issue of jobs. Another possibility is to work through the state legislatures to pressure them to decide the issue, rather than placing the question on the ballot of a general election. Such a strategy would require "looping back" in the analysis to understand the behavior of the state legislatures.

Each of these stakeholder strategies rests only on the objective of getting a particular stakeholder to be more cooperative or less competitive. There is no guarantee that the strategies fit together into one consistent package. Integration is the task for the final phase of analysis.

Phase 5. Define an Integrated
Corporate Stakeholder Strategy

Stakeholder Management is based on corporate adoption of an integrated strategy or set of strategies that deal with the entire stakeholder environment. Sometimes no options will exist except to address specific stakeholders independently. However, to the extent that resources can be used to address multiple stakeholder issues simultaneously, the cost-benefits of this tack become increasingly attractive.

In addition to the cost advantages of an integrated strategy for managing stakeholder relations, there is the additional advantage that inconsistencies in corporate postures among stakeholders are less likely to occur. For example, suppose the USBA had decided to adopt an independent strategy for working with the EPA, promising in it to work for industry pollution-control programs. This would clearly have created major stress in the USBA's relations with its industrial coalition, and would probably have induced the manufacturers to leave the Association in a cross fire between two mutually inconsistent postures.

There are two possible methods of formulating integrated stakeholder strategies. One alternative is to pool all the strategies that are designed for individual stakeholders and try to synthesize the common threads into a "metastrategy" for global management of the environment. In our example, such an analysis might require repeating this activity a number of times to ensure consistency across stakeholders. We can, however, offer a tentative strategy. Ask yourself: What is important to the strategies of dealing with the can manufacturers, brewers, glass bottle manufacturers, retailers, and labor? Answer: The *validity* of the economic argument. But what is important to government officials considering regulatory or legislative options? Answer: The *believability* of the industry's statements about economic arguments.

This suggests an interesting integrated strategy. The USBA could commission a totally unbiased study conducted by an independent third party to assess the true aggregate cost of forcing a change to an all-returnable-container system. The study could then be extended to assess the costs of dealing with the problems through approaches other than legislation; that is, through municipal solid-waste-recovery systems, cost-efficient litter cleanup, and so forth. The second, so-called "free-market cost" ought to be lower than the first, so-called "forced-change cost." If it isn't, the industry should be willing to convert to the mandated system voluntarily.

Assuming the free-market cost is considerably lower than the forced-change cost, the USBA could initiate a voluntary "set-aside" program equal to the difference between free-market cost and forced-choice cost. These funds would be used to support the startup of businesses to efficiently deal with the problems. Members of the industry would contribute to the fund in proportion to the damage they would suffer through the less efficient forced-change solution.

This systemic solution has many potential advantages. First, the industry is seen as addressing the problem with a responsible alternative. Second, the beverage industry could avoid arguments with its opposition about whether the industry had overstated the economics of a forced-change conversion, because it is acting on the opposition's information; that is, if it overestimated the cost of forced conversion, it would have unnecessarily increased its contribution to the set-aside program. Third, everyone in the industry should gain by this action as compared with the alternative. The critical hurdle the USBA must overcome to implement this strategy is convincing all affected parties that if no initiatives are taken by the industry, the forced-change costs would probably be imposed through government legislation or regulation. Tracking industry sentiment and proper timing of proposals become critical to success here.

The second technique for creating integrated strategies is to work directly from the explanatory analysis of individual stakeholder behaviors. This approach attempts to identify common threads in behaviors that can be capitalized upon through redesigned corporate stakeholder strategies. For example, it's critical to the success of the USBA's position that resources be invested in new canning technologies. Otherwise, there will be a de facto erosion of the economic position of these containers, and legislation restricting their use will be more likely. Understanding the reasons behind each stakeholder's position with respect to the support of new can technologies must facilitate new strategy designs by the USBA. For example, the EPA and the environmental groups would want to encourage such technology if they thought it would be directed at reducing litter, pollution, energy consumption, and solid waste. Can manufacturers would be willing to devote resources to such efforts if they were sure a profitable market for their product would emerge. Brewers would support such efforts if it facilitated overall market growth and didn't hurt this group's own competitive position.

As a third party, the USBA may be able to create an integrated proposal that gives each party assurances of achieving its objectives without causing conflict. One such possibility would be special economic credits from the government for ecologically superior containers, plus guaranteed market access for any product that met certain ecological standards.

Each approach to building integrated stakeholder strategies has its own advantages. By integrating the individual stakeholder strategies, the process is relatively efficient, because the new strategy has been assembled from individual strategies. On the other hand, strategies developed directly from behavioral analyses may imply additional options that would not have been part of any individual stakeholder strategy, and thus might have been missed by integrating strategies directly.

Under the right conditions, the beverage container industry might have developed an integrated strategy that would have avoided a showdown of polarized options. A coalition of industry, government, and environmental forces might have been created to develop and use more ecologically desirable containers. Government tax incentives with industry pledges to take lower profit margins on such containers could have fostered this effort. As things turned out, several promising R&D efforts in this direction, such as the Basic Materials Super-Stuff container, were substantially scaled back, because of fears that the investment would never have a market. A classic lose–lose outcome resulted.

The final step of the strategy integration process is perhaps the most important one. The organization must reexamine whether it is committed to each of the objectives identified initially. If any of the objectives causes major stakeholder conflicts, is the organization committed to maintaining the objective under the pressure it creates? Fundamentally, the organization must ask itself how much it is willing to fight a hostile environment in order to achieve the things it believes are important. In some cases the company must be willing to make changes within its own house.

Assessment

When can we learn from the preceding analysis of the USBA's stakeholder management problem? Clearly there were some alternative strategies that the USBA could have adopted. Stakeholder Management systematically draws out less obvious strategic options and helps managers establish a more diverse range of thinking—the kind that is essential if one is to effectively and creatively manage the external environment.

I chose the USBA case to illustrate the details of the Stakeholder Management process because it was a rich and complex problem and it involved many groups that had an impact on the final results. The process is designed to help bring order and control out of confusion.

Does Stakeholder Management really deliver the goods? Would it have worked in practice for the USBA, or is the preceding illustration a good rationalization of the facts based on 20–20 hindsight? For a hint at the answer, let's turn to a case in which a company actually enacted the process on a pilot basis.

New England Telephone

Perhaps no industry faces more day-to-day pressure in making decisions under the conflicting demands of diverse stakeholder groups than the public utilities. These companies are hybrid organizations, obligated to serve their shareholders, but at the mercy of public utility commissions to obtain rate increases for the services they provide. The battle scars and war stories of managing these organizations could fill volumes. Utility executives have experienced firsthand nearly all the problems that can arise when the stakeholder system starts to get out of control.

In 1978 a group of executives at New England Telephone Company (NET), a subsidiary of AT&T, applied Stakeholder Management to a pressing management problem. The executives were excited by the potential the process offered and committed the company to test its usefulness.

One of the problems confronting New England Telephone in 1978 was the increasing cost of providing free service for local directory assistance calls. The pricing procedure NET used was to average the total cost of directory assistance across all customer bills. Essentially, customers who made no calls for information paid for the calls of those who made more than average use of directory assistance. In addition, the volume of directory assistance calls for numbers already listed in the directory was climbing steadily.

New England Telephone reviewed the situation and saw an opportunity to maintain its basic low-cost phone service by separating regular service from the specialized directory assistance service. Calculations showed that by implementing a Directory Assistance Repricing (DAR) plan in Massachusetts, the company could save roughly $20 million a year.

Prior to filing the DAR plan with the Massachusetts Department of Public Utilities (DPU), the company announced its intentions during an annual stockholders' meeting. With the announcement rose a ground swell of opposition, led by the company's union leadership, which foresaw a loss of operator jobs under DAR. As a result, the Massachusetts legislature promulgated a bill prohibiting New England Telephone from introducing a DAR plan in Massachusetts for one year and mandating that the DPU hold public hearings on the issue.

Faced with these decisions, NET management decided that a more positive, aggressive approach was needed. A middle-level manager was appointed "Project Manager for Stakeholder Management of DAR," housed in the public relations department. He reported to the manager responsible for relations with the DPU.

A three-phase program was undertaken: (1) contacting stakeholders and establishing a dialog, (2) choosing a specific DAR plan, and (3) formulating an implementation strategy. The basic stakeholder strategy was to involve stakeholders early and to establish a two-way dialog before the public hearings would take place.

Initially, NET identified more than 25 stakeholders. The list, however, was cut down to 16 key groups that could have an impact on the DPU or the state legislature and that would exercise "yes–no" control over any DAR plan presented. Groups such as the Better Business Bureau, Chamber of Commerce, Bay State Council for the Blind, Office of Deafness to the Massachusetts Council for Older Americans, Massachusetts Consumers' Council, and Local 2222 of the International Brotherhood of Electrical Workers constituted this list of core stakeholders.

Management contacted each stakeholder for its sentiments on a DAR plan and began to build some cooperative relationships. Open-ended dialogs were held with virtually all key groups. Little opposition to the DAR concept surfaced from these discussions, and after NET demonstrated a willingness to take stakeholder concerns into account—for instance, to grant exemptions to handicapped users unable to consult the telephone directory—pockets of positive support started to form. A public survey commissioned by the company showed support for the concept by consumers at large. One key reason for this was NET's decision to include in its plan a provision to refund to customers all the revenues generated by DAR. The savings realized over time would be used to defer future rate increases.

Particularly important during this dialog phase was the union's refusal to negotiate on DAR. Directory assistance is a labor-intensive service. Given the rapid rate of substitution of capital for labor in the industry, the union used DAR as an issue on which to go to the mat with NET management. The company offered to guarantee alternative jobs to all personnel affected by the proposed plan, but the union wouldn't budge. Thus the company knew that ultimately the issue would be decided in the state legislature, which was pro-labor. Therefore the company believed the public hearings would be critical.

Two key stakeholders testified at the legislative hearings— the union and a consumer group "Fair Share," which had a history of opposing utilities in Massachusetts. After subsequent meetings with NET management, Fair Share did not testify at DPU hearings. Press coverage of the issue was favorable to NET's cause, and no organized opposition materialized at the first two DPU public hearings.

Nevertheless, the state legislature passed the bill banning DAR. Massachusetts Governor Edward King vetoed the bill but was overridden by both houses of the legislature. In the final vote in the state senate, the bill was sustained by a single vote.

Although they lost the battle, New England Telephone's managers were not caught with their pants down as events unfolded, nor were they swallowed up in a crisis atmosphere. Bridges were built, and a more cooperative stakeholder environment was created for future issues. Management understood very well the need to manage an issue well in advance of formal public proceedings.

NET's management realized that it cannot always create a short-term win–win solution within a complex external environment. Though the company thought that a job guarantee for those affected by DAR would create a win–win solution, the union disagreed. Ultimately, the state legislative hearings turned into a win–lose situation, and the company lost. The case clearly demonstrates the need for integration across management functions so that all stakeholder relations are effectively covered. The NET project manager worked with diverse groups within the company—Public Affairs, Consumer Affairs, Labor Relations, Rates, and Public Relations. He also kept top management abreast of volatile issues.

The New England Telephone case illustrates an important point: Employees are *not* under management's control. This group must be treated as part of the stakeholder environment, not as a body that will fall in line whenever managers pull some strings.

It is ironic that New England Telephone lost its battle because it could not get the union on its side. The union was the group with which NET might have expected to have the easiest time establishing a meaningful negotiative dialog, since the vehicle for communication with this group was already established. But the problems with this relationship obviously ran far deeper than the DAR issue.

The severity of AT&T's national labor problems was evident in mid-1979, when the Communications Workers of America designated June 15 as "job pressure day." Through public demonstrations, labor hoped to generate enough external support to force the Bell System to take steps to alleviate pressures that create job dissatisfaction.[5]

AT&T had already recognized the approaching squeeze. Six months earlier the company had created a "work relationship unit" to assess the impact of societal changes on Bell's employee relations and to propose relevant policy changes.

Considering AT&T's national labor problems, New England Telephone's stakeholder management strategy had little chance to dramatically reverse that climate in just a few short months. NET's senior executives realized this, and despite the fact that the DAR results went against the company, they committed themselves to continue the approach. The need to get the employees into the company's corner is obvious: Nearly one out of every hundred U.S. workers is employed by the phone company. AT&T's employees represent an exceedingly powerful stakeholder if they can be mobilized on a given issue. Company executives now realize this and are taking appropriate actions.

Other Applications

To formalize the Stakeholder Management process requires a relatively large commitment of time and resources. However, the turbulence of the external environment and the impact that stakeholder relations can have on organizational performance make the risk of committing to the stakeholder approach small compared with its potential payoff.

Stakeholder Management need not be restricted to formal systems in order to pay off. Nor need it be applied only to problems that relate to groups outside the company. As pointed out earlier, the approach has at least as much applicability for managers trying to get a strategy moving *within* the company. Getting agreement among organizational units that are threatened by the potential implications of a "radical" idea requires as much skill as does negotiating with external groups. Stakeholder Management can be a powerful tool for enabling a manager to get an idea accepted.

Unfortunately, many managers don't work out a selling strategy, and their good ideas die in the debates that follow. A few hours of analysis to depict stakeholder relationships and develop strategies to create strong coalitions can make the difference between getting a good idea implemented and seeing it buried.

In this sense Stakeholder Management is a tool for the politics of management. A good manager intuitively goes through many of the steps in the stakeholder process, whether dealing with an internal or an external issue. Effective implementation requires a sensitivity to both favorable and unfavorable forces.

The political realities of decision making in any large organization are that tradeoffs, negotiations, and compromises are always the rules of the game. A quick mental check of the steps in the Stakeholder Management process can help ensure more favorable solutions. Followed properly, such an approach can help minimize the chances that good ideas that might really make a difference to organizational performance will get lost in endless discussion.

Obviously the Stakeholder Management process involves a substantially different level and degree of commitment to problems of the external environment than does advocacy advertising. Stakeholder Management is a complicated and time-consuming process. Further, it implies a new orientation and a substantially different foundation for management. I believe, however, that this type of investment is required if executives are to have a full understanding of all the interdependent factors that must be considered in developing corporate strategies. *The most significant problems corporations are facing today can be solved only if we are willing to consider such fundamental change.*

Toward an Integrated Methodology

So far we have examined two key concepts as possible vehicles for increasing corporate innovation and for getting new ideas implemented—Strategic Assumptions Analysis and Stakeholder Management. In the final chapter we'll look at how these concepts can be integrated into a unified management process—and how that process can work.

REFERENCES

1. "Business on a Soapbox," *Media and Marketing Decisions*, June 1979, p. 64.

2. "The Corporate Image: PR to the Rescue," *Business Week*, January 22, 1979, p. 46.

3. Steinman, J., *Beer Marketers' Insights* (industry newsletter), West Nyack, N.Y., 1977.

4. Ibid.

5. "The Dissatisfaction at AT&T," *Business Week*, June 25, 1979, p. 91.

7

An Integrated Approach to Strategic Innovation

*The optimist proclaims that we live in the best of all possible worlds;
the pessimist fears that this is so.* —JAMES BRANCH CABELL

Strategic Assumptions Analysis and Stakeholder Management rest on a number of common principles for encouraging innovation:

- Both enable active leadership in the innovation process by executives who collectively possess the knowledge and experience to assess complex situations and shape priorities.
- Each is a participative, group-oriented process whereby executives with divergent orientations and perspectives resolve differences of opinion through an organized interchange of ideas.
- The methodologies require quantification of the key consensus judgments that produce the final strategy, enabling staff groups to gather the facts that confirm or refute solutions.
- They are ongoing managerial processes that produce strategies to be refined or revised whenever information shows a change in conditions that were assumed to be valid when the strategy was formulated.

In spite of their similarities, the two processes attack the problem of building corporate strategies from fundamentally different positions. Strategic Assumptions Analysis produces solutions that *fit well* into the environment in which they must be implemented. Stakeholder Management, on the other hand, enables executives to develop strategies that *change* the corporation's business environment into one of greater harmony with the company's objectives.

The contrasting objectives of the two methods can create a dilemma in applying them to specific problems. Some problems are best suited to an approach that utilizes Strategic Assumptions Analysis; others require a Stakeholder Management orientation. Must a corporation invest resources in learning to use both processes and then, based on the nature of the problem it faces, judge which route is most appropriate? Both methodologies are designed as ongoing *management processes,* not as mere stopgap, shot-in-the-arm techniques implemented on a moment's notice to salvage the organization from one-time crises. To achieve full effectiveness, these broad-based, sustained decision processes must become integral parts of the management system. Likewise, the company's organizational structure, its operating procedures, and its support systems must simultaneously be compatible with the integrated process. An organization cannot operate with two approaches, even if the processes have common underpinnings.

Fortunately, since the two methodologies can be integrated into a unified process, it is not necessary to choose between them. Let's examine how they can be synthesized.

Integrating the Approaches

In describing the integrated methodology, two distinct issues need to be addressed: (1) the problem/opportunity resolution, that is, determining the steps in the process that yield more innovative solutions to specific key management concerns, and (2) the organizational process, or determining how the methodology relates to the normal roles and responsibilities of people in the organization. Both the product issue (problem solving) and the process issue (organization) must be addressed in a balanced way in order to produce an effective methodology.

Improvements in organizational processes are necessary in order to provide better ongoing problem-solving capabilities. But there is an important difference in how managers will treat priorities for improving organizational process versus better problem-solving methods. Most managers support corporate efforts to achieve better organizational processes, but few will invest their own time in such activities unless they believe the effort will have a clear and direct impact on the resolution of a problem of immediate concern to them. Hence, in order to have any real benefit, an organizationwide management process must possess an associated problem-solving capability. An explanation of the integrated methodology begins by describing the steps of the approach.

Dealing with Strategic Issues

Many of the most significant changes in corporate strategies emanate in an unplanned way as executives respond to the problems and opportunities they encounter. The event that triggers such changes can be almost anything that is important enough to attract executive attention. For example, the stimulus might be an unanticipated initiative by a competitor, an opportunity to buy a business, an R&D breakthrough, or a labor strike. The question to be addressed in such situations is: How does the company ensure that it does not merely react to the specific triggering event with a mechanical, timeworn response when a broader perspective on the problem and an innovative approach are really called for?

Figure 23 illustrates a ten-step offensive response to a trigger issue that incorporates both Strategic Assumptions Analysis and Stakeholder Management concepts. Let's briefly analyze each step.*

Step 1. Pure Strategy Options

The first step is identical to the initial stage of Strategic Assumptions Analysis. All the reasons for initiating SAA with a creative brainstorming session to generate plausible solutions apply here. The most compelling of these reasons is the need to design a problem-solving process that is compatible with the natural inclinations of good managers; that is, to move to workable solutions as quickly as possible. This trait can and ought to be capitalized upon in any process that is established to optimize the time investment of talented people.

Step 2. Implied Corporate Objective

Nearly all companies have a list of expressed objectives. Unfortunately, this list is often written in such generalities that it provides little guidance for the clarifying actions managers ought to take when faced with specific problems or opportunities. As a result, the objectives usually have little impact on managerial behavior.

An alternative process for defining objectives and determining priorities for them is to examine the objectives implied by the proposed solutions to the problem at hand. This activity can provide managers with far-reaching insights and may lead to a modification of either objectives or strategies. The key element of this process is to make strategies and objectives

---

* For a complete outline of the ten-step offensive response, see the Appendix.

Figure 23. Inducing innovation in corporate response to problems or opportunities.

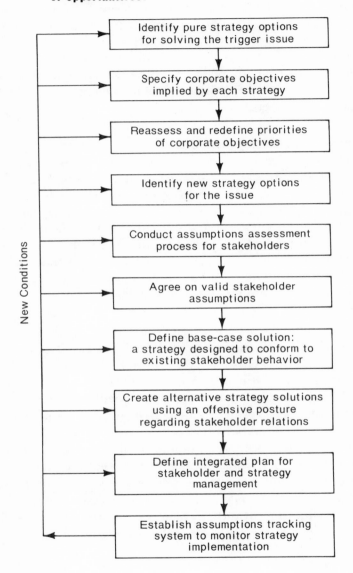

consistent. Questions such as "What does this strategy say about our commitment to product quality?" and "What does this strategy imply about our human resources development objectives?" can reveal otherwise overlooked plausible solutions.

Step 3. Priorities of Objectives

With the expanded list of possible objectives that the activities of Step 2 generated, the executive group must now decide which objectives it believes are valid and the relative importance of them. The Beliefs Assessment process described in Chapter 5 is appropriate for accomplishing this task. Because the objectives that have been generated from the strategy options are likely to be considerably more specific and controversial than those an executive group usually addresses, the discussion is likely to be insightful in evaluating the identified objectives. The issue is to reach agreement on the organization's commitments as exemplified by its *actions*, rather than by its aspirations.

Step 4. Additional Strategy Options

To the extent that a reassessment of objectives leads to an improved perspective on corporate priorities, the executive team is likely to have some new thoughts on how to address the key problem. This time, however, the solutions are generated with direct reference to the company's objectives. Solutions are designed to conform to the objectives of the company; that is, the *ends* to be achieved are used to develop *means* for solving a problem. Theoretically, this is how management always formulates strategies; in practice, however, the strategy-building process seldom evolves as planned. Because of this newly initiated reference of thinking, more innovative solutions are likely to emerge from the process.

Step 5. Stakeholder Assumptions Assessment

Using the assumptions-assessment methodology of SAA, the group can now examine the assumptions that underlie each of the strategy options it has developed. The benefits of a systematic, stakeholder-by-stakeholder assessment of key behaviors required for the strategy to succeed were discussed in Chapter 6. They all apply to the stakeholder/strategy process as well.

Step 6. Valid Assumptions

Using the SAA methodology to assess the validity of the assumptions, the group must agree on a set of assumptions it is willing to accept about each key stakeholder. Its members will then have a picture of the environment in which they will probably respond to the key problem or opportunity.

Step 7. Base-Case Solution

Using the issue analysis process developed in Chapter 4, the group formulates a strategy that best fits the accepted assumptions about stakeholder behaviors. This strategy should succeed if the assessments are accurate; that is, the consequences of implementing the strategy ought to be accurately forecasted and evaluated as to their acceptability.

Step 8. Offensive Stakeholder Strategies

By applying the principles of Stakeholder Management, a second class of solutions can be developed. Rather than accept the base-case assumptions about stakeholder behaviors, strategies are developed to remove the stumbling blocks represented by those groups whose actions thwart the achievement of better results. More cooperative behaviors of each of these groups are identified and reasons why such actions might be realized are specified. Stakeholder Strategies are then developed to achieve the desired change.

Step 9. Integrated Plan

The group is now in a position to describe how to spend its resources to solve the problem or exploit the opportunity. If the cost-benefit relationship of the offensive stakeholder strategies is judged to be too low, the base-case solution would be adopted. If there are salient advantages to trying to change the environment for the better, the Stakeholder Management approach would be adopted. In either case, managers must assess explicitly the risks and returns of broad or narrow definitions of the problem. This activity minimizes the chances of getting trapped into a view of a problem that is either too constrained to be effective or too ambitious to be implemented.

Step 10. Assumptions Tracking

Once the group has defined the best strategy, it can assemble all the key stakeholder and environmental assumptions that are critical to its success. These assumptions provide the bases for an information tracking system to ensure there is no major change in the validity of these positions. If the tracking system signals a change in status, appropriate reviews of the steps and strategy conclusions will be undertaken.

Changing Organizational Processes

The key advantage of a methodology that integrates the Strategic Assumptions Analysis and Stakeholder Management processes is that it forces an organization constantly to examine the tradeoffs between plausible ways in which its resources may be used. Executives always have the option either to work within the external environment as it exists or to try to change it. By forcing an explicit examination of both options, there may be less tendency for managers to just shake their heads in disgust over the "hopeless" state of the environment. Instead of accepting these conditions and trying to muddle along doing "as well as possible under the circumstances," there may be more challenges to the constraints. Some problems that are currently solved by strategies designed to *minimize losses* may be turned into opportunities that *maximize advantages*.

The proposed stakeholder/strategy process focuses on a related management problem: The various strategies a company may adopt to deal with the divergent issues it faces can easily create conflicting postures in its relations with key stakeholders. For example, a company's programs to reduce its operating costs certainly alienates employees as jobs are phased out, and thus undermines employee-relations programs designed to motivate workers to take more pride in their role in fostering company success. Witness the struggles of the auto and housing industries to maintain jobs during business slumps, when sales of big-ticket items are the first to crumble, and worker motivation in those sectors is not far behind.

Similarly, marketing strategies designed to capture business from competitors may be initiated at the same time that industry associations comprising the same competitors are developing programs to fight government legislation. Or business may fight government regulation on basic free-market principles, while the removal of specific government mechanisms to protect markets or prices is resisted.

The problems of balancing the conflicts created by divergent corporate actions cannot be avoided. But the dilemma must be recognized as far as possible before such strategies are undertaken. A stakeholder group usually forms one overall impression of a corporation based on the long-term interactions it has with the organization. Success in one program can go out the window if relations in others are bungled.

Undoubtedly, the greatest challenge in the design of organizational processes to support the stakeholder/strategy methodology is the effective coordination of stakeholder relations and corporate strategies. I'm not aware of any corporation that is structured in such a way that it can always accomplish this balancing act, because few companies treat the stakeholder dimension as an integral and continuing aspect of corporate strategy formulation. Traditionally, public affairs departments have undertaken the bulk of corporations' stakeholder relations. As a result, public affairs strategies—using either media campaigns or direct responses to stakeholder inquiries and complaints—are usually ineffective in solving basic problems with stakeholder groups. But because public affairs seldom contribute substantially to the formulation of corporate strategies, the efforts of this department fall far short of the demands of the stakeholder/strategy process.

Even for stakeholder groups important enough to warrant a special corporate function, such as employee relations or corporate relations, the management process is usually ineffective for the proposed process. Although employee and corporate relations groups may have a better understanding of the stakeholder behaviors related to their function, their inputs into the creation of corporate strategy are usually minimal. Instead, they respond to the strategies *after* they have been formulated, creating programs to execute them in their areas of responsibility. What doesn't occur is the input and dialog required to shape a corporate strategy that makes sense from all stakeholder perspectives.

Three elements are required to make the integrated stakeholder/strategy process work smoothly:

- *Permanent groups must be established that have a continuing responsibility to offensively manage the relations with specific stakeholders.* That is, they must maintain information systems that explain the attitudes, objectives, and behaviors of a stakeholder; and they must implement offensive programs for improving the cooperative posture of the stakeholder group.

- *Flexible team-oriented resources groups must be available to concentrate on solutions to specific problems and opportunities as they arise.* Team size and composition are determined by the complexity of the issue and the diversity of experience and perspectives necessary to assemble and analyze all the relevant factors. The teams are not permanent, but rather remain active only until a strategy is developed and approved.

- *A permanent top-management policy group must be organized to assess risks and establish priorities among strategies and stakeholders.* In resolving specific tradeoffs, this group would constantly reassess corporate objectives in order to provide guidance to functional groups as they develop ongoing plans and programs in their areas of responsibility.

Although it may be possible to modify traditional organizational structures to achieve these three elements, another approach to their success is to redesign the organization from scratch to fit its needs. Let's examine such an alternative structure.

Stakeholder/Strategy Matrix Organization

As has been discussed, a key element of the stakeholder/strategy process is that it enables management to expose and successfully resolve conflicts inherent in the formulation of corporate strategies. This situation immediately suggests a matrix structure of management, which is designed to highlight areas of potential conflict. Although a matrix management system is more complicated to administer than a conventional product-line or functional organizational structure, it is gaining popularity in management circles. This is because a matrix system forces the important conflicts to the top of the organization, where the best perspective should exist for their resolution.

Most matrix structures are designed to separate the "classic" points of conflict in an organization. For example, one dimension may be product lines and another functional activities. This particular structure would force tradeoffs in the use of R&D or production department resources (the functional units) among the various products that are sold.

Matrix management principles can be readily applied to the design issues in the stakeholder/strategy process. Figure 24 illustrates the two dimensions to the matrix system and identifies the three key functions that occur in the management process. Through such a system, the roles and responsibilities for making the process work become apparent. *Stakeholder managers* must know how each strategy impacts on the relations with a particular stakeholder; they consolidate stakeholder relations across all strategies. The *strategy task forces* analyze the impact of each stakeholder's behavior on possible strategies for solving a problem or achieving an opportunity; they consolidate strategy consequences across all stakeholders. Each dimension of this system is like the head or tail of a coin: The outcome of the perfect flip—edgewise—integrates the balanced, complementary inputs of both sides.

The heart of the process occurs in the strategy/stakeholder interactions. When Stakeholder Management is established as a continuing function, rich strategic issues should emerge rather quickly, because the Stakeholder Management system is continuously developed and refined, rather than assembled from scratch when a stakeholder crisis arises. This means that the tradeoffs and evaluations being made will be complex and wide ranging. The judgments are not likely to be easy, but it is difficult to argue against having to make the judgments explicitly. In most situations today they are made implicitly by default; that is, they usually aren't even considered.

Suppose a corporation were to make a commitment to adopt

Figure 24. A matrix organization for a stakeholder/strategy management process.

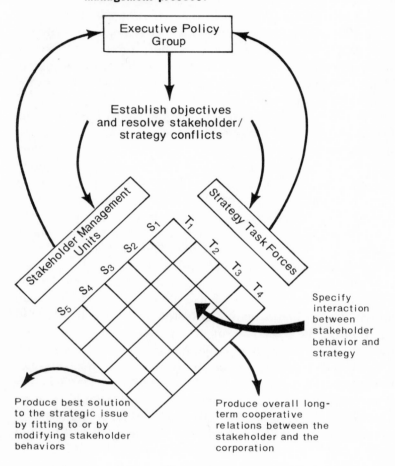

the stakeholder/strategy process and to implement the matrix management organization. What would happen to the traditional organizational structure of each operating department? These groups would still probably exist, but their functions would change substantially. They would have an operating, rather than a strategic, focus in the organization, maintaining the vital ongoing logistics functions that are essential to the overall health of the company. But issues of strategy—the long-range fit between the organization, what it sees as its basic missions, and how it intends to accomplish them—would be undertaken through the stakeholder/strategy process. The link between the logistics functions and the strategy process would be accomplished by involving personnel from both areas on the Strategy Task Force.

These are the fundamental, but not the only, necessary changes. Let's examine some of the less apparent management implications of the stakeholder/strategy process.

Required Managerial Posture

Successful implementation of the stakeholder/strategy process requires a basic reevaluation of management style and philosophy. A fundamental change in management's decision process without a corresponding assessment of management style completes only half the task. For most organizations the reevaluation is likely to produce a number of changes. Many of these changes will depend on the unique situation in the particular company. However, four features of current management are likely to require reexamination in nearly all those companies.

Develop a Generalized Marketing Approach

A key to the success of a stakeholder manager in the matrix organization is the ability to assemble information that provides an understanding of stakeholders' behaviors. For the company's customers, the basis for doing this is likely to be already in place. Modern marketing is based on the principle of understanding consumer behavior, and market research methodologies have been established to provide the needed knowledge. Indeed, few companies would implement product marketing strategies without first developing a significant body of research on consumer needs.

But equivalent processes of market research to justify company strategies oriented toward other stakeholders are often nonexistent. Internal conflicts, such as territorial perspectives, often prevent the application of sound marketing principles to the external environment. Market research is channeled only toward the needs of the customer, and "marketing" to such stakeholders as environmental and civil rights activists is often confined to advertising special programs or corporate image, with few intellectual exchanges made on vital issues. Significant corporate decisions are often made about these groups with almost no understanding of their objectives or constraints.

The basic marketing principles that govern a corporation's strategies for its customers can and must be applied to each of the other major stakeholders. Each stakeholder manager must operate in an organizational environment that parallels the activities now undertaken by the marketing manager. In other words, the marketing concept must be generalized.

Define a Stakeholder Negotiation Process

Understanding stakeholder behavior through a marketing-oriented process is only a part of the picture stakeholder managers face. The role also calls for action; in this case, action means negotiating with stakeholders.

Most organizations see issues in the external environment as threats to the status quo; if a consumer group wins, then the company must lose. But this reasoning is often shortsighted; there are often no-lose situations, as well as win–lose and no-win situations. The management of General Motors saw Ralph Nader's "Campaign GM" as a win–lose situation. Their actions, or more accurately, their *reactions*, allowed Campaign

GM to receive more publicity and did more to erode GM's image than negotiation could have. In fact, years later GM has implemented some portion of every one of Campaign GM's original proxy statements.

Five crucial activities must be understood if negotiations with stakeholders are to be successful:

Information collection
Information dissemination
Bargaining on specific issues
Coalition formation
Unilateral action

Information collection is important because it improves the understanding of each stakeholder's position. Without such information collection procedures, misperceptions drive ineffective strategies, as we saw in the U.S. Brewers Association's misreading of public concerns about litter in the returnable-container issue.

Information dissemination is equally important. Just as it is essential for the corporation to understand the objectives of its stakeholders, it is equally critical for stakeholders to understand the corporation's position. This does not mean that business must reveal trade secrets or disclose strategic decisions, but that it must understand the principles of negotiation.

The importance of information collection and dissemination was demonstrated indirectly in a major Wharton School study done some years ago for the Arms Control and Disarmament Agency.[1] Research to define causes of conflict escalation and deescalation showed that in conflict situations people and organizations act on a variation of the Golden Rule, namely, "Do unto others as you *believe* they would have done unto you." Valid information about both parties, the study concluded, is critical to the creation and implementation of mutually acceptable solutions. If misperceptions or ambiguities exist, each side will tend slightly to bias its beliefs by assuming less cooperative motivations on the part of the other parties. Matching this position reinforces the notion that the conflict is real. The net result is often a spiral into a serious conflict situation, all because the original positions of each side were not well understood by the other.

A notable example of the foul-ups that can result from the failure to perform these information functions adequately is the Spring 1979 accidental leak of radiation into the atmosphere from the Three Mile Island nuclear power plant in Pennsylvania. During the first hours of the crisis, conflicting information about the dangers of the accident found its way to the media. Thereafter, the credibility of further reports was damaged. But more important, the information function was not carried out well during the critical time period—*before there was an accident.* Key stakeholder groups knew little about nuclear energy. The public, with little concrete knowledge of the risks involved, was most in the dark; it was greatly surprised and deeply concerned by the accident. In just a few days, the momentum of public opinion shifted from a state of relative neutrality and nonconcern to one of widespread criticism of nuclear power.

By exercising the appropriate information functions earlier, the nuclear utility industry would not have escaped the searching policy questions now being asked; but the industry could have debated the questions in an atmosphere free of tension and with a much stronger negotiating position than it now has. Neither "slick PR" nor silence is strategically feasible. Honest dialog with appropriate stakeholder representatives is crucial if we are to avoid future conflicts of this type.

The third key activity in successful negotiations is the negotiation process itself. Each organization must make proposals and counterproposals to identify feasible solutions. By doing this, each party can try to create no-lose situations, which cannot occur if the conflict escalates beyond control.

The fourth activity is the understanding and forming of coalitions. An organization or stakeholder can often join forces with another stakeholder to strengthen each group's position in relation to some third party. Since coalitions are illegal in such business practices as setting prices, corporations have a tendency to retreat from forming alliances even on issues for which there are no legal constraints. Businesses need not act in isolation or solely in conjunction with other businesses.

Finally, the organization must consider the effect of unilateral actions, in which it adopts an independent strategy with some expectations as to each stakeholder's response. The Wharton conflict study referred to above showed that such actions have a high potential for escalating the conflict and thus should be used cautiously. Yet most organizations manage their stakeholder relations almost exclusively through unilateral, defensive actions. They collect and disseminate little *useful* information, negotiate only when forced, and treat each stakeholder and issue separately. This often resulted in the adoption of strategic responses that are haphazard. Procedures should be established so that the full range of negotiation options is considered and appropriately used. These procedures must be understood and accepted by senior management. Otherwise, stakeholder managers will be forced to operate in an ad hoc, fragmented, jerky fashion. This situation can destroy management credibility and will ultimately lead to failure of the function.

Establish a Risk-Taking Management Philosophy

Risk is critical to the success of the entire management process; it is necessary in order to achieve effectiveness for both the stakeholder management and the strategy task force dimensions of the matrix. The commitment to risk taking, however, can come only from the highest echelons of the organization.

Many successful organizations take the initiative with their customers; risk-taking behavior with this stakeholder group is a natural part of business. But for many of the other stakeholders, the organization is defensive; it reacts only when forced to by explicit initiatives from the stakeholder. When action is required in these situations, the objective is usually to return the environment to the state before the "disturbance" arose by neutralizing stakeholder initiatives.

The reasons for executives adopting a reactive posture to stakeholders other than the customers are easy to understand. The consequences of an inappropriate negotiation strategy with one of these stakeholders are highly visible and can be costly. On the other hand, a successful strategy is never seen by those at the top because it *prevents* a problem from occurring. Hence most managers adopt the "safer" risk-avoidance course—thus sustaining the status quo—rather than enact strategies that carry risks in an atmosphere absent of explicit outside intimidations.

A risk-avoidance posture results in short-term, myopic perspectives that ignore the early warning signals of future conflicts, and actually increases the chance that such conflicts will materialize. More important, this stance greatly reduces the organization's opportunity to control the eventual outcome of the conflict in order to achieve jointly satisfactory results with the external stakeholders. Thus a short-term, risk-avoidance, reactive posture—characteristic of most organizations today—should be replaced by a long-term, risk-taking, offensive posture.

Successful implementation of this philosophy in an organization originates with the issue of how managerial performance is evaluated. Safeguards must be established to ensure that managers make decisions based on all the *real* costs, benefits, and risks of actions and strategies, not merely the *visible* ones. If actions are taken based on visible costs alone, then a reactive and short-term focus will almost certainly result. Such a focus usually forces the company to take unilateral action when the problem reaches such a state of crisis that something must be done. If there has been no previous communication, the crisis escalates.

To prevent such crises and to achieve this "success factor," senior management must be presented with all the expected consequences of action *and* inaction in dealing with stakeholders. One example of taking an offensive posture toward stakeholders is the recent move by some public utilities to create open dialog sessions with consumerists. Joint panels have been established with consumer leaders to discuss issues before managerial decisions are made. Some companies have gone even further and formed top-level Consumer Affairs Committees with responsibility for understanding the needs of consumers and how the company can help satisfy them. One company even sponsored a conference of consumerists, government managers, and academics to solicit their views on a major strategic issue. Of course, such actions have an element of risk, but the benefits—increased credibility and more viable business strategies—are often well worth the vulnerability they entail.

Redesign the Resources Allocation Process

Management processes in business organizations typically revolve around the traditional perspective of the organization's function, that is, the optimization of the supply–conversion–selling activities. Most companies are organized on either a product-line business-line basis or a functional basis. Product management is separated from external relationships, and each area is in turn separated into discrete elements. Because of this, the information needed to build integrated stakeholder strategies does not surface at a central place in the organization. Therefore, appropriate resources are never committed among stakeholders.

Typically, the functional organization devotes too much of its resources to such highly visible stakeholders and too little to such stakeholders as special-interest groups, which are no one's direct responsibility. The key problem is that the traditional forms of organization discourage a systematic perspective on the stakeholder environment. Without this perspective, the resources required to keep the stakeholder system in balance will probably not be properly allocated, and crises in various parts of the system will continue to occur. The focus on fire fighting in specific areas must be redirected if the stakeholder process is to be realized in practice. To achieve this, the resources allocation process must be redesigned.

The stakeholder/strategy matrix organization provides the basis for such a reallocation. But the process of deciding how to budget resources for the various activities is much more complex than with most traditional systems. This is because none of the activities is directly tied to a revenue or profit base. As a result, financial returns can be used only indirectly to make assessments. Furthermore, appropriate levels of allocation may shift dramatically as situations change and new priorities are established. Senior management will be forced to assess the specific merits of each investment option in detail in order to make intelligent decisions. The process is likely to be time consuming and complicated. Nevertheless, it is vital that it be undertaken, because resources allocation decisions are at the heart of establishing corporate priorities.

The Challenges of Change

The pace of American industry is increasingly in the hands of major corporations, all of them vast and complex organizations. If a leader of one of these institutions were convinced that fundamental changes in decision-making processes are required to ensure the future survival of the company, where should the executive start?

Two elements are essential for accomplishing change of this magnitude. First, there must be a clear, well-defined vision of what the organization ought to be like when the change process is completed. Second, there must be a systematic step-by-step plan for moving the organization from its current operating posture to the desired state. Neither of these elements is easy to obtain. Few top executives have the time necessary to generate their own vision for long-term changes in organizational processes. Many are completely overloaded simply trying to make intelligent responses to short-term crises.

The writing of this book has been partly an effort to help executives create a vision for the future. Even with widespread acceptance, however, neither this nor any other "third-party-created" vision can provide a complete perspective for a corporation's future direction. From my experience, the commitment to make a fundamental change in the organization will occur only after the key executives invest the time to create their own visions. Outsiders can provide good inputs to the process, but not shortcuts through it. Executive time involved in the design is absolutely essential for success.

As difficult as it may be for a corporate executive to free his time and resources from the constraints of day-to-day matters to formulate a desired organizational design, the development of a workable plan for getting there is likely to be even more challenging. There are a number of significant pressures that will be operating when any plan is being implemented, any one of which could scuttle the entire mission. Let's look at three of the more significant pressures that will have to be neutralized if a plan is to work.

Transition Period Pressure

The offensive plan must be formulated as a sequence of programs designed to move the organization systematically from one style of management and organization to another.

This is far different from a program of specific problem solving, which represents a short-term response to specific difficulties in a particular segment of the management system. The greatest difference is that a planned change of the entire system implies that there will be a transition period in which the management process is partly new and partly old. As a result, during this time it is very likely that the overall effectiveness of the system will be worse than the system it is meant to replace.

As the managerial process deteriorates during the transition period, pressure to abandon the new plan will increase. Constant questioning from many quarters about whether the "new look" is a flawed design that can't work will emerge. Obviously, one cannot be blind to such a possibility. But if the change is worth attaining, then resources will be required to see things through the rough times. It's like pushing a rock up a small hill to get it rolling down a large mountain: If you don't have the energy to get it over the hump, the rock will roll back to its original spot—and perhaps even overtake those who were trying to propel it.

The key to relieving transition pressures is a plan that is properly timed and sequenced. At a time when the organization is operating in a short-term crisis mode, one would be ill advised to commit resources to an effort that is guaranteed to make things worse. Furthermore, by closely examining elements that are part of the change, it is possible to stage the activities in such a way that disruptions are minimized. To achieve this coordination, however, the plan must be very carefully designed, and its implementation must be closely controlled by the executives who initiate it.

Pressures on Organizational Culture

More and more managers recognize that there are factors under their control that can either encourage or inhibit the organization's acceptance of change. This has led to a new field of management research called "process consultation," which deals with strategies to accomplish change more effectively. At this point, however, more is known about the problems of organizational resistance to change than about ways to overcome these problems.

This situation can create a serious roadblock to a program designed to fundamentally change organizational processes. Many people who are in key positions and "know the ropes" of the existing system will be threatened by the implications of the program. If they aren't supportive of the new design, they are in a position to sabotage its successful development. And they can almost always do so in ways that executives never realize are happening.

For example, the most prominent reason that programs to "clean up the federal bureaucracy" usually fail is resistance to change among civil servants. Often, proposals for bureaucratic improvements are logically designed, but the system they are meant to improve is so complex that only those people on the inside know how it really works. As a result, these insiders can make or break a proposal for change. Usually they undermine it because it threatens their power bases. The control that those inside an organization have over the success or failure of attempts to change occurs de facto. Therefore, any plan for changing the system must have built-in processes to obtain the support of these people. In short, the people in the organization must participate in redesigning it so that they have a stake in the new design. Success takes time and requires mutual trust, but that trust cannot be abbreviated if the program is to have a chance to succeed.

Time Pressure

Finally, the offensive action plan will require the organization to resolve the issue of executive time required to implement the plan. None of the current role pressures on corporate executives will disappear; in fact, they are likely to intensify. Where will the time come from to orchestrate this program? The responsibility cannot be delegated to others, because only senior executives have the full organizational perspective required to assess whether the program's pace and emphasis are appropriate.

Too often the issue of executive time availability is ignored when programs of fundamental long-term change are initiated. "If it's important enough, we'll make the time available" is often the answer when the issue is raised. In my experience, unless there is explicit consideration given to how the time will be generated, it probably won't become available. The enormous pressure to respond to short-term crises almost always takes precedence over the time allotted to long-term projects that have less clear goals and deadlines.

I witnessed the time allocation dilemma in one consulting project for a corporation that wanted to institute a meaningful long-range business plan. The client had no explicit programs for long-range growth prior to the planning effort; executives spent all their time in day-to-day management of the existing business. The new endeavor ground to a halt when the executives realized they could not possibly manage the normal operational activities of the business and also direct the programs that were intended to generate future growth. Thus the long-range programs were halted, and a new effort was begun to develop more sophisticated management support systems that would enable the executives to manage day-to-day operations with greater efficiency. Such a program should have been started before any new business development strategies were even considered.

The issue of pressure on executive time provides the same message as does the issue of pressures during the transition period and pressures on the organizational culture: If the overall implementation plan isn't carefully designed to recognize these problems and incorporate solutions to them, the entire effort can crumble. Any one of these pitfalls can be devastating to a plan for change if it is not treated explicitly. In short, committing to the plan is a high-risk situation: Few things can go smoothly; many can go asunder.

The Leaders Must Choose

Everything I've presented can be synthesized into one fundamental question: Are the payoffs for trying new approaches to management worth the inherent risks and resource investment they require? Obviously, I think they are. In the final analysis, however, the issue will be decided by the leaders of American industry. They will reap the rewards or suffer the losses for the postures they adopt. The decisions we currently face are difficult ones, but I believe our economic system will produce the correct answers. Presently, American business is facing a serious challenge to itself and to the social and political structures it supports. We face enormous problems because of limited resources and energy, growing competition on world markets, rapidly evolving technological expansion among competing nations, and changing public attitudes about the role of business in society. Yet this is not the first time that the American business leadership has faced serious issues. In the past, innovative leaders showed us the way out of economic and psychological depression and toward new levels of performance and productivity. I believe the leaders of American business will rise to the occasion again.

Perhaps the most important ingredient in our process of generating the best solutions to our long-term problems is a sustained, healthy dialog on the complex issues and our options for dealing with them. It is in this spirit of creative risk that I have undertaken, with this writing, to provide one starting point toward a solution. If the challenges raised and the approaches presented here help managers clarify their own perspectives on better foundations for our management system, I shall have achieved my objective. The important thing is that we maintain an insatiable hunger for ever-improving answers to our myriad problems. Otherwise the system as we know it faces slow—and certain—decay. We cannot allow that to happen.

REFERENCE

1. Emshoff, J. R., *Analysis of Behavioral Systems.* New York: Macmillan (1971).

Appendix:
The Stakeholder/Strategy
Process

Terms and numbers in parentheses refer, where appropriate, to the relevant step in the Strategic Assumptions Analysis or the Stakeholder Management process, and to the page(s) where a description of the step appears in the text.

Step 1. **Define pure strategy options (SAA 1, pp. 86–89).**
       a. Identify, through discussion, basic strategy options.
       b. Identify advocacy team for each strategy option.
Step 2. **Specify corporate objectives (SM 1, pp. 148–150).**
       a. Identify objectives implied by each strategy option.
Step 3. **Prioritize objectives (SAA 3, pp. 93–95, 107–108).**
       a. Using Beliefs Assessment, assess validity and relative importance of each implied corporate objective.
Step 4. **Identify additional strategy options (SAA 4, pp. 95–96).**
       a. Collect all uncertain objectives.
       b. Negate uncertain objectives.
       c. Develop additional options.
       d. Recycle through Steps 2, 3, and 4, until no more additional strategy options are forthcoming.
Step 5. **Assess stakeholder assumptions (SAA 2–3, pp. 89–95).**
       a. Identify stakeholders.
       b. List stakeholder assumptions that support each strategy option.

201

    c. List environmental assumptions that support each strategy option.

    d. Test assumptions for relevance (negation process).

    e. Organize stakeholder assumptions according to levels of generality.

Step 6. Identify valid assumptions (SAA 5, pp. 107–108).

    a. Using Beliefs Assessment, develop a pool of acceptable, valid assumptions about each stakeholder, as a basis for understanding the environment in which the problem exists.

Step 7. Define base-case solution (SAA 6, pp. 99–103).

    a. Using the issue analysis process, identify issues important to the problem.

    b. Analyze assumptions about each issue, based on yes–no questions.

    c. Determine overall management posture on each issue.

    d. Define base-case strategy.

    e. Evaluate "costs" of conditional assumptions.

    f. Revise base-case strategy.

Step 8. Develop offensive stakeholder strategy options (SM 2–SM 5, pp. 150–166).

    a. Explain actual, cooperative, and competitive behaviors for each stakeholder.

    b. Using Beliefs Assessment, assess the certainty of the validity of these explanations.

    c. Identify direct- or indirect-strategy options for inducing more cooperative or less competitive stakeholder behaviors.

Step 9. Develop an integrated plan (Chapter 7).

    a. Assess costs and benefits of base-case and offensive stakeholder solutions.

    b. If stakeholder approach generates a cost-benefit relationship that is too low, adopt the base-case solution.

    c. But if the base-case solution is found to be less attractive, adopt the offensive stakeholder solution.

    d. Assess the risks and rewards of the resulting broad or narrow definitions of the problem.

Step 10. Establish Assumption Tracking System (SAA 7, pp. 103–104).

    a. Identify key assumptions that support the validity of the plan.

    b. Identify information that will test the validity of the assumptions.

    c. Establish tracking system to collect information about assumptions and report exceptions to management.

    d. Reassess strategy as exceptions arise.

Index

205

THE
WORLD OF
ANTIQUES, ART,
AND ARCHITECTURE
IN VICTORIAN AMERICA

Robert Bishop
and Patricia Coblentz

E. P. Dutton   New York

(Above). *A Victorian Idyll*, artist unknown. New Jersey. 1850–1860. Oil on canvas. 20″ x 26″. The Victorian gentleman who commissioned this portrait of his Gothic Revival house was understandably proud of all he possessed: a commodious home in the latest fashion dominating broad lawns with flowering urns, tree roses, rustic furniture, a many-tiered fountain, his child driving a goat cart, and a large greenhouse in the background. (Private collection)